Library of
Davidson College

Essays in Comparative Sociology

Essays in Comparative Sociology

ANDRÉ BÉTEILLE

New Enlarged Edition

DELHI
OXFORD UNIVERSITY PRESS
BOMBAY CALCUTTA MADRAS
1987

Oxford University Press, Walton Street, Oxford OX2 6DP
New York Toronto
Delhi Bombay Calcutta Madras Karachi
Petaling Jaya Singapore Hong Kong Tokyo
Nairobi Dar es Salaam
Melbourne Auckland
and associates in
Beirut Berlin Ibadan Nicosia

© Oxford University Press 1974, 1987

First published in 1974 and
reprinted three times as
'Six Essays in Comparative Sociology'

New enlarged edition 1987, entitled
'Essays in Comparative Sociology'

SBN 19 562145 X

Filmset at South End Typographics, Pondicherry
Printed at Crescent Printing Works Pvt. Ltd., New Delhi 110001
Published by S. K. Mookerjee, Oxford University Press
YMCA Library Building, Jai Singh Road, New Delhi 110001

TO MY FATHER

TO MY FATHER

Preface to the First Edition

In September 1972 I was invited by the University Grants Commission to deliver the National Lectures in Sociology for 1972-73. This book is an outcome of that invitation.

My initial plan was to write a set of three lectures and to deliver them at three universities. After I had written the third lecture—in January 1973—I felt I needed to write three more in order to reveal more clearly the connexions among the first three and to relate the whole effort to the concerns of sociology in contemporary India. The first three essays were delivered as lectures at Chandigarh, Aligarh and Lucknow. The fourth and fifth were never really delivered as lectures. The sixth is based on a lecture that I have given from time to time to students in the Department of Sociology at the University of Delhi.

The first essay looks backward; the last, I hope, is forward looking. I doubt if in the years to come many serious students of society in India will worry greatly about the distinction between sociology and social anthropology except as a problem in academic administration or academic politics. But I do believe that Indian sociologists must increasingly come to terms with Marxists who are also students of society but with a different perspective. So far they have behaved towards each other rather like half-brothers; each has pretended, at least in public, to be more or less unaware of the other's existence. As I see it, there are certain fundamental differences between Marxism and academic sociology which it will be very hard to resolve; but there is also much common ground between the two. Sociology has no doctrine to defend, hence sociologists need have little fear of losing their faith by being exposed to Marxism.

This is my second exercise in comparative sociology; the first was a selection of readings on social inequality which I edited for Penguin Books. Indian sociologists have by and large fought shy of doing comparative sociology, but have provided raw materials to others interested in pursuing cross-cultural studies.

There are special reasons why Indians have confined themselves mainly to the study of their own society. They have far fewer resources for studying other societies and cultures than have American or European scholars. Yet I believe it to be not only possible but also fruitful for Indians to work in the framework of comparative sociology while keeping India at the centre of their minds. In contributing to comparative sociology, Indians will have to look increasingly to neighbouring countries like China, Pakistan and Bangladesh.

I am grateful to many people for their stimulation in the preparation of these essays, and especially to Jit Uberoi from whom I have learnt much in the course of our close and somewhat contentious association. I was treated with much kindness at the three universities which I visited for delivering the National Lectures. My special thanks are due to Professor V. S. D'Souza, his colleagues and students at the Department of Sociology, Panjab University; to Professor R. N. Saksena, his colleagues and students at the Department of Sociology, Aligarh Muslim University; and to Dr. K. S. Mathur, his colleagues and students at the Department of Anthropology, Lucknow University.

Finally, I would like to thank the University Grants Commission for inviting me to deliver the first series of National Lectures in Sociology—an undeserved honour which I gratefully acknowledge.

André Béteille

Preface to the Second Edition

A somewhat thoughtless choice of title for the first edition of *Six Essays in Comparative Sociology* has required the publication of the second edition under a new title. Two new essays have been added and two notes in the form of appendices to two of the chapters previously published. Nothing has been omitted of what was published in the first edition, the six essays of that edition reappearing here in their original form.

The two new essays, which appear as chapters 7 and 8, both deal with Marxism which was the subject of the concluding chapter, entitled 'Marxism and Modern Sociology', of the first edition. Chapter 7, 'Marxism, Pluralism and Orthodoxy', was delivered as the M. N. Roy Memorial lecture in New Delhi on 22 March 1982 and published in that form by the Indian Renaissance Institute; it is republished here by courtesy of the Institute. Chapter 8, 'Is There a Marxist Anthropology?' was presented as a keynote address to the Association of Social Anthropologists on 5 July 1983 on the occasion of its Third Decennial Conference at Cambridge; it has not been previously published. The two appendices were both published previously in the *International Social Science Journal*, 'Sociology and Ethnosociology' in vol. 26, no. 4 (1974), and 'On the Concept of Tribe' in vol. 32, no. 4 (1980); they are reproduced here with the authorization of the Editor.

A.B.

Contents

	Preface to the First Edition	vii
	Preface to the Second Edition	ix
1	Sociology and Social Anthropology	1
2	Peasant Studies and their Significance	23
3	The Concept of Peasant Society	42
4	Tribe and Peasantry	60
5	Peasants and Workers	82
6	Marxism and Modern Sociology	101
7	Marxism, Pluralism and Orthodoxy	118
8	Is there a Marxist Anthropology?	141
	Index	167

1
Sociology and Social Anthropology

IT IS USEFUL to examine the relationship between sociology and social anthropology as it has taken shape during the last few decades in order to see more clearly the work being done by scholars in these fields in India today. Most textbooks devote a few paragraphs to the topic, but the discussion is generally presented in somewhat abstract, and even ideal, terms. A purely formal discussion of the subject will not be very useful any longer: a discussion at this stage will serve a purpose only if it creates a deeper awareness of the work in which we are actually engaged.

Contrary to what they say, academics are much preoccupied with labels. But if our discussion is to be fruitful we must look into the reality that lies behind the labels. Are the investigations made by sociologists and social anthropologists basically similar or are they basically different? If they are basically similar, then why divide the investigators into two categories and draw an artificial line between them? If they are basically different, then why not maintain the distinction between them consistently and why are people, particularly in India, continually changing roles, appearing now as sociologists and again as social anthropologists? We should take a critical look at the prevailing division of work among students of human society and culture.

One might feel that ideally this division of work ought to be the same throughout the world; but we know that in reality this is not the case. The relationship between sociology and social anthropology is not the same in France as in Britain, and the difference was greater sixty years ago. Anglophone countries have, on the whole, maintained a distinction between the two, and this distinction was at its sharpest in the period between the two World Wars. The division of labour between sociology and social anthropology emerged in Britain or the United States under specific historical conditions, and was then transmitted to other countries where conditions were different. There is no ground to believe that what appeared reasonable and appropriate under certain conditions will always appear to be so.

A proper division of work among students of human society can be established only on the basis of their ultimate academic objectives and their actual academic concerns. But in dealing with the relationship between sociology and social anthropology we are faced not only with academic distinctions but also with administrative divisions. In the administrative sense this relationship is already established when a university or a research institution decides to regard the two as the same or as different. It is beyond the scope of the present discussion to review the administrative organization of the social sciences in India. But clearly, the division of labour among scholars should be governed ultimately by academic and not by administrative considerations.

In India sociology and social anthropology as academic disciplines are of relatively recent growth. The first university departments were started at Bombay and Calcutta a little over fifty years ago, but the real growth in their organization began only after Independence. This is in a sense fortunate for it means that the pattern of administrative organization that has emerged has barely had time to acquire a rigid form. This makes it particularly appropriate to examine now the rationale of the division of labour that is taking shape.

In examining the relationship between sociology and social anthropology we must begin by recognizing that there is no single conception of either. We must not forget that as recently as thirty years ago anthropologists were sharply divided about their basic frame of reference even within the Anglo-American tradition. British anthropologists, following largely the lead of Radcliffe-Brown, regarded social structure as their basic field of interest, while Americans were more in favour of the study of culture.[1] While this

[1] For the British point of view see R. Firth, 'Contemporary British Social Anthropology', *American Anthropologist*, Vol. 53, pp. 474–90, 1951; for the American point of view see G. P. Murdock, 'British Social Anthropology', *American Anthropologist*, Vol. 53, pp. 465–73, 1951.

particular debate has died down—and in retrospect appears to have been rather fruitless—other differences may still be observed.

The European way of looking at the subject has been somewhat different again. In Europe the term anthropology has generally been used in a restricted sense to refer only to physical anthropology, whereas what the British and the Americans referred to as social and cultural anthropology was broadly described as ethnology. As Radcliffe-Brown pointed out many years ago, social anthropology and ethnology did not have identical orientations.[2]

It is necessary to point out that we are dealing here with differences not only in labels but also in contents. Those who described their work as ethnology or as cultural anthropology felt justified in investigating both material and non-material culture. In Britain, on the other hand, the change from the phase of ethnology to that of social anthropology was accompanied by a quiet withdrawal of interest from the study of material culture. Now, it does make a difference whether or not we consider the study of the material culture of a people as essential to an understanding of their social institutions.

In turning to sociology in the restricted sense, we are struck no less by the different ways in which sociologists have conceived their subject. About forty years ago Karl Mannheim wrote two essays, one on American sociology and the other on German sociology, in which he constrasted the empiricism of the former with the philosophical preoccupations of the latter.[3] On the whole, the Anglo-Saxons have a different approach to sociology from the Europeans, and when they feel particularly ill at ease with European sociology, they tend to characterize it as social philosophy, or just philosophy.

To add to this, we now have Soviet sociology which defines itself in opposition to 'bourgeois sociology'.[4] The history of sociology in the Soviet Union is in itself a subject which calls for separate treatment. Although it had its origins at the turn of the century, it did not find a fertile field for development in Russia after the Revolution. In its present form it is of relatively recent origin—going back not more than twenty years—and it is perhaps too early to say what shape it will eventually acquire.

---

[2] A. R. Radcliffe-Brown, 'The Methods of Ethnology and Social Anthropology' in M. N. Srinivas (ed.), *Method in Social Anthropology, Selected Essays by A. R. Radcliffe-Brown*, Asia, 1960.

[3] Karl Mannheim, 'American Sociology' and 'German Sociology (1917–1933)' in *Essays in Sociology and Social Psychology*, Routledge and Kegan Paul, 1953.

[4] For a representative example see G. Osipov, *Sociology*, Progress Publishers, 1969.

So much diversity in the conception of what is sociology and what is social anthropology may be a sign of vitality, but it can also become a source of confusion. If one wishes to assert the fundamental unity of the two subjects, a particular conception of sociology can be chosen and it can be shown to be the same as the prevailing conception of social anthropology. But by choosing another conception of sociology someone else can highlight not the similarities between the two subjects but their differences. Which conception of sociology or of social anthropology one prefers will in turn depend on how the relationship between the two is viewed.

This brings us to a consideration of the difference between principle and practice, between what people believe or declare to be their ultimate objective and what they actually do. There is no reason to think that in the social sciences, any more than in other spheres of social life, there will be perfect correspondence between the two.

It might happen that two sets of people define their ultimate objectives in very different terms, but in actual practice engage in much the same kind of work. Thus, in spite of their very different basic orientations, there might be much in common between Soviet and American sociologists in the work they actually do. On the other hand—and this is what concerns us more—people might define their broad objectives in the same terms but actually work in very different ways. I would argue that sociology and social anthropology have similar or even identical aims, and yet sociologists and social anthropologists have often done very different kinds of work.

The comparative study of social interaction and of social institutions became fairly well-established in Europe and America by the beginning of the present century. The stimulus to this kind of study was provided by the growing awareness that the methods of science could be properly applied to the study of social facts. Social life was seen to have patterns, and the exploration of these patterns became the principal concern of a number of scholars who were initially recruited from a variety of disciplines.

There were two aspects of these studies which gave them a distinctive character from the very beginning, and which continue to be their defining features even today. The first is a general sense of the inter relatedness of the different institutions of a society. Some scholars have emphasized some institutions more than others, but they have all sought to view society as a system, however loosely integrated. The second is the application, in some form or other, of what I would call the comparative method. Again, some scholars have sought to make broader generalizations than others, but they have all acknowledged the utility of comparing institutions of various societies in order to reveal their similarities and differences.

Now if we define sociology in this way, we will see at once that it can serve equally well for a definition of social anthropology. This indeed was the argument of Radcliffe-Brown who maintained that social anthropology was the same as comparative sociology. As is well known, Radcliffe-Brown enjoyed great prestige among social anthropologists in the English-speaking countries, and one of his pupils, W. Lloyd Warner, occupied a pre-eminent position among American sociologists in the thirties and forties. But despite the logic of Radcliffe-Brown's argument, sociologists and social anthropologists remained for the most part divided in their work in countries such as Britain, the United States, Australia and Canada.

If we are to understand why Radcliffe-Brown's logic made so little headway against established habits, we must find out how these habits came to be established. Sociology and social anthropology had both begun by asking general questions about the nature and origins of human society as a whole. They became scientific disciplines only when they began to make empirical investigations into particular societies. Now the types of societies social anthropologists and sociologists chose to study in detail were from the start very different from each other. Thus, it is an irony that in Britain and America the very process that transferred the study of society from the plane of philosophical speculation to that of scientific investigation also led to an increasing divergence between sociology and social anthropology.

Despite Radcliffe-Brown's admonitions, in Britain social anthropology became in effect the study of primitive, pre-literate or tribal societies in the colonies instead of developing into comparative sociology in the full sense of the term. Radcliffe-Brown's own empirical investigations were made among the Andaman Islanders and the Australian aborigines, and his comparisons were comparisons of the institutions of tribal societies. Malinowski did not go even so far as that; his writings were based almost wholly on his fieldwork in the Trobriand Islands.

Malinowski's pupils worked mainly in Africa where they investigated the institutions of a variety of tribal societies. These investigations brought out in a vivid way the manifold interrelations among the different institutions of particular societies, and in this way contributed much to the understanding of the basic principles of social life. There were also comparative studies of politics, kinship and cosmology among African tribes. These detailed studies of tribal life—both particular and general—besides contributing to theory, were also of some practical value to colonial administrators.

George Homans pointed out some years ago, with some exaggeration, that students of human society in Britain seemed to believe that the only societies requiring scientific study were those of the native tribes, but never their own.[5] It was for this reason, he said, that Britain had produced outstanding anthropologists but no sociologist. While this might not be altogether fair, it certainly drew attention to the fact that in Britain a sociologist would be a person who studied British society or societies of the British kind; and in general he would be a very different person from one who studied native societies.

Colonial rule inevitably projects the view that the institutions and customs of the ruling country are fundamentally different from those of the colonies. The distinction between those who study their own society and those who study other cultures is one reflection of this view. It is no accident that it reached its peak at the height of the colonial regime. With the end of this regime, sociologists and social anthropologists are beginning to come closer to each other in Britain.

Colonial rule is not the only condition which highlights the differences between societies. In the United States this condition was provided primarily by the co-existence of two very different kinds of social and cultural systems within the same country. No contrast could be sharper than the one between the complex, technologically-advanced and aggressive civilization of the industrial cities and the pre-literate, technologically-backward and moribund culture of the tribal reservations. It is out of this contrast that the distinction was born in the United States between sociology and social or cultural anthropology.

The great American anthropologists of the first half of the twentieth century—Boas, Kroeber, Lowie—all concentrated on the study of American Indian tribes. These tribes were for the most part isolated in reservations where they lived under special conditions.

[5] G. C. Homans, 'Giving a Dog a Bad Name' in G. C. Homans, *Sentiments and Activities*, Routledge and Kegan Paul, 1962.

These conditions differed not only from those in the industrial cities but also from the conditions under which the American Indians had lived before the Europeans came. The reason why American anthropologists at first concentrated on the study of culture traits is that the people they studied had for the most part ceased to have ongoing social systems of the kind which could be observed by British social anthropologists in Africa.[6]

The ongoing social systems studied by the Americans were those which were taking shape in the rapidly expanding industrial cities. Americans have not shown the kind of inhibition about examining their own society that Homans says he found among the British. On the contrary, they have produced a larger volume of empirical investigations than has been produced by sociologists in any other part of the world. Further, until recently American sociologists have been preoccupied with the study of their own society to the virtual exclusion of all other societies.

The city has loomed large in the investigations of American sociologists. As is well known, the strength of American sociology—like that of British social anthropology—has been its grounding in empirical research. The problems of work and management in factory and office, of leisure and recreation in the home and neighbourhood, the different sectors of the city and their socio-economic characteristics—it is the study of these that has given to American sociology its distinctive shape. By contrast rural sociology has always been a low-priority and low-prestige subject in the United States.

Primitive and civilized societies came to be studied by different sets of scholars on the view that they were very different from each other. These differences were real and not imaginary, although they were probably exaggerated by the manner in which the study of social life came to be organized. When all societies are studied within the framework of a single discipline one is likely to regard them as variants of the same basic pattern. When their study becomes divided between separate disciplines, one is more likely to regard them as representing basically different patterns.

If social anthropologists have paid much attention to the study of kinship systems, it is because these systems *are* so much more

---

[6] A similar point has been made by Max Gluckman, *Politics, Law and Ritual in Tribal Societies*, Basil Blackwell, 1965, pp. 33–4.

conspicuous and pervasive in tribal as opposed to industrial societies. Where, as among the Australian aborigines, the entire community can be represented on a single genealogy, the study of genealogies and the values attached to genealogical ties naturally becomes important.

Again, when four separate terms are used for describing cousins, this naturally becomes a subject of interest to the investigator in whose own society only a single term is used. The collection and analysis of kinship terms by the genealogical method has been since the time of Rivers an essential part of the training of every anthropologist. By contrast, the study of kinship and marriage—as distinct from family relations—has been of little concern among sociologists, particularly in the United States. When Homans embarked on a study of preferential kin marriage, he felt he was playing the role of an anthropologist, which was something unusual in an American sociologist.[7]

What the study of kinship was to anthropology, the study of social class or stratification was to sociology. Here also the approach to the problem differed somewhat between European and American sociologists. The former were more concerned with the study of class in the Marxian sense; the concerns of the latter centred more generally around prestige and social ranking. The anthropologist showed little interest in these problems because the tribal societies he studied did not generally have either clearly graded strata or mutually opposed classes.

Studies of kinship on the one hand and of stratification on the other have generated highly specialized bodies of literature, each having its own methodology, its own array of concepts and its own technical vocabulary. This difference is clearly reflected in the contents of professional journals, particularly in America. Not many sociologists today feel they have the competence to contribute to or even follow the current discussions in the field of kinship theory; similarly, most anthropologists would be baffled by the subtleties of the techniques being developed for the study of social stratification. This is in a way unfortunate because the problems of kinship and of social inequality are of general if not universal significance to students of human society.

Tribal and industrial societies represent two extremes, whether we view them on an evolutionary scale or simply arrange them

---

[7] G. C. Homans, 'Introduction', op. cit.

according to size and complexity of structure. In the West anthropologists have been particularly attracted to the most primitive or elementary forms, and sociologists to the most advanced or complex forms of human society. If either or both had chosen to work on middle ground, the differences we see between them might not have emerged. As we have remarked, historical factors played an important part in leading them to choose societies whose differences were more manifest than their similarities.

Given this fundamental difference in the point of departure for empirical inquiries, other differences were bound to develop. But these are of secondary importance. We have already observed that there are differences in the institutional areas typically emphasized by sociologists and social anthropologists, but these in themselves are not what matter. When someone studies kinship and marriage in a New York suburb he can claim to be a sociologist; but when he studies status and rank among the Kwakiutl Indians he will be regarded as an anthropologist. In America—and to some extent also in Britain—what really counts is the kind of society one investigates, not which aspect of it one analyses.

Again, while sociologists and social anthropologists in Britain and America tend to use different sets of concepts, it would be a mistake to regard this as the basic source of their difference. Differences in the conceptual apparatus became more pronounced the more definitely scholars began to concentrate on empirical studies of opposite kinds of society. And in spite of this, basic concepts such as 'structure', 'function', 'status', 'role', 'conflict', 'change' and 'evolution' continue to be used in much the same way by sociologists and social anthropologists.

Much has been made of the differences in method used by students of the two varieties of human society. However, firstly, these differences are not as large as they are often made to appear. Secondly, no field of scientific inquiry can be defined by its method. What is of fundamental importance is the problem; it is the problem of study which should determine the method to be used. I would go further and distinguish between approach, method and technique, and say that sociology and social anthropology have the same approach to the study of social life, that their methods are similar, but that they have developed different techniques of investigation and analysis.

The contrast between anthropology and sociology is often drawn in terms of the opposition between the methods of intensive fieldwork and of survey research. This way of making a contrast appears to be empirically false and logically untenable. No sociologist interested in the study of real societies would like to deny himself the possibility of doing intensive fieldwork; no anthropologist would like to exclude in principle the possibility of doing survey research.

Intensive fieldwork is particularly suited to the requirements of studying pre-literate tribal societies. A Western scholar who wishes to collect data on tribal life has to travel a great distance to make his observations. If an Englishman, he has to leave his country and travel to Africa or Melanesia or Australia. If an American, he has to travel at least from his urban home to a reservation. This itself is a major investment, and one who makes it would naturally like to stay in the field long enough to be able to get a reasonable return on it. Those who have seen British anthropologists preparing to set out for fieldwork in Africa can understand why they seek to remain in the field for at least a year.

There are other reasons why the anthropologist needs to spend a long time in the field. If he is to collect reliable data he must learn the local language; the sociologist already knows this, since in Britain and America he usually studies his own society. The anthropologist not only must learn a new language but has also to make himself familiar with new categories of thought. In this way he collects his data and ensures that they are reliable and meaningful. All this makes it essential for him to proceed with patience and care. Other techniques of investigation can be applied only after the anthropologist has got his bearings straight through the method of intensive fieldwork.

In Britain and America sociologists study the working of institutions with whose basic nature they are to some extent already familiar. Hence they can afford to miss the preliminary step of getting acquainted with an unfamiliar culture. But clearly, this is only a matter of degree. In a complex industrial society there are many compartments, and when a sociologist seeks to probe into one which is very different from those in which he has grown up, he too must start with intensive fieldwork. William Foote Whyte has described how the world of an American slum was so different from his own middle class environment that in order to study it he was compelled to use the method of intensive fieldwork.[8]

[8] William F. Whyte, *Street Corner Society*, University of Chicago Press, 1955, Appendix.

These considerations have led some to reformulate the distinction between anthropology and sociology in slightly different terms. It has been said that anthropology is the study of 'other cultures', implying that sociology is basically the study of one's own society and culture. Lévi-Strauss has emphasized the differences of perspective in the study of one's own as opposed to alien institutions.[9]

But this way of making a distinction can lead only to confusion. For if applied consistently, what anthropology is to an American will be sociology to an Indian, and what sociology is to an American will be anthropology to an Indian. The distinction will work only so long as all societies, Western and non-Western, are studied only by Western scholars. It becomes meaningless when scholars from all over the world begin to study their own as well as other societies.

If the arrangement of work among students of society in Britain and America is a response to a particular set of conditions, then we can expect a different arrangement in countries where the conditions are different or are perceived differently. However, there are many complicating factors. Habits of work among scholars might persist even when the conditions which gave rise to them have changed. Further, habits of work which originate in one country might be transmitted to another even though they are quite inappropriate to the conditions there.

It would be wrong to suggest that colonialism necessarily creates a dichotomy between anthropology and sociology, as happened to a large extent in Britain. If we turn to France which also had a colonial empire we will find a somewhat different pattern of relationship between students of primitive and of civilized societies. This relationship has changed between the end of the last century and the present time. If in France at a certain stage the study of all types of human societies became part of the same intellectual endeavour, this probably happened despite the colonial reality which divided the world into two. But the reality soon made its presence felt, so that in France perhaps even more than in Britain the study of primitive and civilized societies are now two different things.

Radcliffe-Brown's idea referred to earlier, that there can be only one science of comparative sociology embracing the study of all human societies, did not in fact originate with him, but with his

---

[9] G. Charbonnier (ed.), *Conversations with Lévi-Strauss*, Jonathan Cape, 1969.

distinguished French predecessor, Émile Durkheim. Durkheim occupies a unique position in the history of sociological thought. He is regarded as a founding father equally by sociologists and by social anthropologists. And he continues to be a source of inspiration to students of human society in every part of the world.

Durkheim not only preached comparative sociology, as so many before and after him have done, but practised it with great distinction. He believed that the same methods should be used for studying all types of societies, and himself applied them to the study of totemism among the Australian aborigines, rates of suicide among contemporary Europeans and forms of solidarity in ancient and modern civilizations. No other student of Western societies had Durkheim's insight into primitive societies, and in this he had few rivals even among the anthropologists of his time.

The true significance of Durkheim's work lies in the fact that it was a product of collective endeavour. Durkheim had collected around himself a band of scholars who shared a certain conception of human society and a certain method of sociological inquiry. They worked in close association with each other and investigated societies of diverse kinds. The results of these investigations were published in the journal *L'Année Sociologique* which stands as a remarkable testimony to the unity of sociology and social anthropology.

The *Année Sociologique* was established in 1898 and discontinued in 1913. It was during this period that the French school of sociology acquired its distinctive shape. Durkheim and his associates were not fieldworkers in the modern sense, and this in a way made it easier for them to discuss a wider range of societies than is generally done today by those who collect their own empirical material: I have mentioned earlier the part played by empirical investigations in bringing about a separation between sociology and social anthropology in Britain and the United States.

Whereas students of human society in the Anglo-Saxon countries were at that time interested mainly in the study of two types of society, the tribal or very primitive and the industrial or very advanced, members of the *Année Sociologique* group were, in addition, interested in the ancient civilizations—Bouglé was a Sanskritist, Granet a Sinologist—and to that extent their outlook was more truly comparative. Their studies make it clear to us today that if the science of society is to be divided according to the types of society being studied, then logically we will need not two but three or more subdivisions.

After Durkheim's death the study of society and culture took a new turn in France. The distinction between sociology and ethnology reasserted itself. In the inter-War years Marxism became a major influence in French sociology and this influence continues to the present time. Durkheim's nephew and collaborator, Marcel Mauss, sought to continue the tradition of the *Année Sociologique*, but his influence remained strong only among ethnologists (or students of primitive and ancient societies) and declined among sociologists (or students of contemporary Western societies).

Today probably the two most influential students of society and culture in France are Raymond Aron and Claude Lévi-Strauss. Their work strikingly exemplifies the separation between sociology and anthropology, the very separation the *Année Sociologique* sought to overcome. Aron is an ardent advocate of comparative sociology, but for him this means in practice the comparison of the variants of industrial society. Lévi-Strauss is also a practitioner of the comparative method, but uses it only for the comparison of primitive societies and cultures. And although Aron began his trilogy[10] on industrial society by holding up *Les Structures élémentaires de la Parenté* as a model of sociological inquiry,[11] he did not make any further reference to the ideas of Lévi-Strauss in the rest of this work.

I have argued that it is one thing to advocate the merits of the comparative method, and another to practise this method in the full sense of the term. In Europe and America there has been a strong tendency to dichotomize the world into the primitive and the civilized, and this tendency has been a more potent factor in determining the actual division of work among students of society and culture than any ideal design for a 'comparative sociology'.

How then should we view the relationship between sociology and social anthropology in contemporary India? We have emphasized at several points the distinction between the ideal designs people construct—whether for the study of primitive or advanced societies, or for a comparative sociology—and the way they actually do their work. A realistic discussion of these two subjects—or these two branches of the same subject—must keep in mind the actual work that sociologists and social anthropologists in India have been doing and are likely to do.

---

[10] Raymond Aron, *Dix-huit Leçons sur la Société industrielle*, Gallimard, 1962; *La Lutte de Classes*, Gallimard, 1964; *Democratie et Totalitarisme*, Gallimard, 1965.

[11] Aron, 1962, op. cit., p. 24.

The first point to note is that both sociology and social anthropology as we know them now were brought to India from outside, particularly from Britain. British scholars who lived in India or came as visitors helped these subjects to get off the ground. Later, Indian scholars trained abroad—mainly in Britain and the U.S.A.— played a leading part in developing studies of society and culture in India. While these scholars added a great deal to our understanding of Indian society and culture, their general theoretical orientations were, with few exceptions, largely those of scholars in Britain and America.

As branches of academic learning, sociology and anthropology were divided almost from the very beginning in their formal set-up in India. They began to be taught as separate subjects in Indian universities a little over fifty years ago. Bombay University started with sociology and Calcutta University with anthropology. For more than two decades these remained the primary centres of teaching and research in the subjects. Later, as new departments came up, universities in the eastern region opted for anthropology and those in the western region generally for sociology. In several of the new universities there are now separate departments for the two subjects although Calcutta has only a Department of Anthropology and Bombay only a Department of Sociology.

Anthropology is usually taught in Faculties of Science whereas sociology is taught in Faculties of Arts (or of Social Sciences). This distinction is carried over into the organization of research institutions and associations. The Indian Science Congress has a section for archaeology and anthropology but none for sociology. There has been since British days an Anthropological Survey of India corresponding to similar organizations in the fields of archaeology, botany, zoology and geology; there never has been an organization of this kind for sociological research.

The division of work that was proposed between anthropology and sociology half a century ago—and is still manifest in much of the formal set-up—reflected in a fairly exact way the distinctions then prevalent in Britain between the two subjects. Anthropologists were to study tribal customs and sociologists were to study the advanced sections of Indian society. It was no accident that W. H. R. Rivers was chosen to be the first head of the Department of Anthropology at Calcutta,[12] and the Department of Sociology at

[12] Rivers did not actually join the Department but died shortly before it was formally established.

Bombay was launched by the urban sociologist, Patrick Geddes. No two students of human society could be further removed in their actual work than Geddes and Rivers.

But whatever the nature of the formal set-up, the actual development of studies in human society and culture followed a different course in India from the ones followed in the West. We have seen how in France the division between ethnology and sociology reasserted itself in spite of the attempts made through the *Année Sociologique* to assert the unity of all studies of society and culture. In India, on the other hand, social anthropologists and sociologists have continually interchanged roles in spite of attempts to separate the two in the formal academic structure.

The vague and arbitrary nature of the line separating the two subjects becomes at once evident when we examine the work done by sociologists and social anthropologists in India. The scholars who have contributed most to the understanding of Indian society and culture are precisely those who have consistently ignored the compartmentalization of Indian society into primitive and advanced sections. This compartmentalization is the true source of the distinction between social anthropology and sociology; once it is set aside, the distinction becomes difficult to sustain.

It is an interesting fact that G. S. Ghurye, who has probably had the longest and most successful career as a Professor of Sociology at an Indian university, was himself trained by the anthropologist, W. H. R. Rivers. The range of Ghurye's interests as well as the continuity between them is best represented in his collection of essays entitled *Anthropo-Sociological Papers*.[13] These essays cover a vast field between dual organization and cross-cousin marriage at one end and the social and economic conditions of clerks in Bombay city at the other.

Ghurye has not only conducted and promoted studies of all sections of contemporary Indian society; he has sought also to examine the basic features of traditional Indian civilization. His book on caste, in its several incarnations,[14] combines interests which in Britain or America would normally be pursued separately by anthropologists, sociologists and historians. In this sense Ghurye's work fits well into the design of the *Année Sociologique*,

---

[13] G. S. Ghurye, *Anthropo-Sociological Papers*, Popular Prakashan, 1963.

[14] Originally published as *Caste and Race in India*, Routledge and Kegan Paul, 1932.

with the difference that the French sociologists were studying societies in all parts of the world whereas Ghurye has confined his interests mainly—though by no means solely—to India.

We find the same combination of interests in the work of N. K. Bose, who occupied broadly the same position among anthropologists at Calcutta as Ghurye does among sociologists at Bombay. Bose had an abiding interest in the tribal people of India, an interest which took him first to the Department of Anthropology at Calcutta University and which he developed later as Director of the Anthropological Survey of India and as Commissioner for Scheduled Castes and Scheduled Tribes. But far from believing that the tribal people of India were so distinctive as to require a separate discipline for their study, he emphasized the essential similarity and continuity between the tribal and the non-tribal people of the subcontinent. And since he was a great believer in the unity of scientific method, he applied the same method to the study of all sections of Indian society, 'primitive' as well as 'advanced'.

Bose's analyses of contemporary Indian society were based on a substantial body of fieldwork. He believed that anthropology was a field science and placed primary emphasis on direct observation in the study of social and cultural life. His fieldwork was, however, rather different from that of contemporary British or American anthropologists. He preferred what may be called extensive as opposed to intensive fieldwork, and felt that this was better suited to the requirements of an Indian social scientist studying different sections of his own society. This enabled Bose to spread his fieldwork over a remarkably wide range: at one end a careful investigation of the Juang tribe of Orissa and at the other a detailed survey of Calcutta city.[15]

The framework of Bose's work is best represented in his book, *Hindu Samajer Garan*.[16] Here again a combination of the perspectives of ethnology, sociology and Indology is revealed. Bose maintained that in order to understand fully any segment of Indian society its relation to the whole design of this society must be seen. Hence the study of tribes in the hills involved the study of castes in

---

[15] His Juang work is described in several of his Bengali and English writings, e.g. *Cultural Anthropology*, Asia, 1961, and *Culture and Society in India*, Asia, 1967; his Calcutta survey was published as *Calcutta 1964, A Social Survey*, Lalvani, 1968.

[16] Now available in an English translation entitled, *The Structure of Hindu Society*, Orient Longmans, 1975.

the plains, just as the study of castes in the villages led to the study of classes in the cities.

The same unity of approach can be observed in the work of the next generation of Indian scholars, notably M. N. Srinivas, S. C. Dube and Ramkrishna Mukherjee. Srinivas, as a pupil first of Ghurye and then of Radcliffe-Brown, has consistently emphasized the unity of social anthropology and sociology.[17] Both Dube and Mukherjee were trained in Departments of Anthropology, but they have both addressed themselves to what would be regarded in the West as properly sociological problems. Dube has studied bureaucracy, communications and the problems of social change in general.[18] Mukherjee has applied sophisticated quantitative techniques to the study of various aspects of Indian society,[19] having earlier contributed to a study of social mobility in Britain.[20]

A historian of ideas writing a hundred years from now might find it strange that students of society and culture in India first set up a distinction between social anthropology and sociology, and then went about almost systematically violating the distinction. We have seen already that the distinction did not originate in this country but was brought to it from outside. We must now examine the specific reasons which make it unworkable in Indian conditions. Only then will we be able to ask whether the distinction itself is logical or not.

The distinction between sociology and social anthropology (or cultural anthropology, or ethnology) thrives on a dichotomous view of the world. Whites and natives, civilized and primitive, us and they: this, historically, has been the basis of the distinction made in the West between the two. But given the way in which Indian society is constituted, it provides very little basis for generating—or sustaining—this kind of dichotomous distinction.

In India, unlike in America or Australia, the distinction between tribal and non-tribal society is vague, unclear and, in the end, arbitrary. If we go by the textbooks, it will be hard to find many groups that conform to the anthropologist's definition of tribe.[21]

[17] His approach is best exemplified in his *Caste in Modern India and Other Essays*, Asia, 1962.
[18] See, for instance, his most recent book, *Explanation and Management of Change*, Tata McGraw-Hill, 1971.
[19] See, for instance, his *The Sociologist and Social Change in India*, Prentice-Hall of India Ltd., 1965.
[20] D. V. Glass (ed.), *Social Mobility in Britain*, Routledge and Kegan Paul, 1954.
[21] For a good example of this see Marshal D. Sahlins, *Tribesmen*, Prentice-Hall, 1968.

The larger Indian tribes like the Santals, Oraons, Bhils and Gonds are certainly very different from the tribes studied by anthropologists in America and Australia. Undoubtedly they had their distinctive customs, but all communities in India, and not just tribes, had and in a sense were encouraged to have distinctive customs.

The larger tribes practise settled agriculture. Their technology is a little more backward and the land they cultivate a little less fertile than of the non-tribal people. Otherwise there is much basic similarity between the two categories of people in their modes of livelihood and economic organization. Clearly, one who has studied an Oraon village in Chota Nagpur does not need to change his discipline when he goes to study a caste-Hindu village in Birbhum district. Indeed it is very likely that he will in the normal course find some non-tribal people in the Chota Nagpur village and some tribal people in the Birbhum village.

The tribal people have been for centuries linked by social, economic and political ties with the non-tribal people of India. This is true of even the remote hill tribes, although in their case the links were generally fewer and not always direct. What N. K. Bose sought to establish should by now be clear to all—that the differences between Juangs, Mundas, Oraons, Oilpressers, Blacksmiths, Weavers and Cultivators are differences of degree and not of kind. We can, of course, for practical purposes, draw a line and separate Juangs, Mundas and Oraons from the others; but we must always remember that the line will be arbitrary and will have significance only for the purpose for which it is drawn.

But if we cannot draw a line near one end, can we not draw it near the other—a line which will separate our emerging urban-industrial society from all that is set in a traditional mould? For surely, the sociologist would wish to prove his mettle by studying not rural society—whether tribal or non-tribal—but the complexities of industrial life in the city. We must see if the Indian city does not provide an altogether different field of investigation, calling for a different approach, a different method, different techniques and different concepts—in short, a different discipline.

But again, we cannot but be struck by the continuities between urban and rural life in India—the urban family and the rural family, city politics and village politics, urban and rural patterns of stratification. After all, it would be surprising if it were otherwise, for city and village have co-existed in India for more than two millennia.

And if industrialization generates new social arrangements—as it undoubtedly does—here too the difference is one of degree rather than of kind. This is why many of those who started by studying rural India, like N. K. Bose or D. N. Majumdar, found it natural at some stage to turn their attention to urban India. If we are to develop a more adequate methodology for urban sociology in India, we will have to build on these beginnings.

We saw earlier that in the West a certain division of work between students of primitive and advanced societies has crystallized into the academic distinction between social (or cultural) anthropology and sociology. In India, in spite of the formal acceptance of this distinction, the actual pattern of work tends to lay stress on the unity of society and of culture. Which of these two patterns of work is the more logical?

It must be said first of all that what we are dealing with is less a disagreement over principle than a difference in patterns of work. Even in regard to actual patterns of work the difference must not be over-stressed. The case of the American sociologist Lloyd Warner, who was a pupil of Radcliffe-Brown, is instructive if not characteristic. He first made a study of the Murngin, an Australian aboriginal tribe, and then applied the lessons learnt in the field to the study of Newburyport, a modern American town.

In more recent times Erving Goffman, who turned from anthropology to sociology, has been an outstanding practitioner of the comparative approach. One could easily multiply examples from both Britain and the United States. But what is really important is that the more closely one examines the matter, the more difficult it becomes to draw a clear line on any logical basis between the two types of investigation into human societies and cultures.

No doubt the argument will continue as to whether there should be one unified discipline of sociology or two separate, though related, disciplines of social anthropology and sociology. Those who argue for a single, unified discipline will agree that the study of various societies will require various techniques of investigation and analysis. And those who maintain that, despite our ultimate aims and objectives, two separate subjects in fact exist and must continue to exist, will in their turn agree that there are very close relations between the two.

My own view is that whether we regard social anthropology and sociology as the same subject, or as different branches of the same subject, or as two different subjects will ultimately depend on how we feel about the varieties of human society and culture. If we feel that the similarities between them are more fundamental than their differences, we will be more inclined to accept the unity of social anthropology and sociology. If, on the other hand, we feel that their differences are more basic than their similarities, we will be more ready to accept the division between the two subjects. I am prepared to concede that there is no more scientific justification for accepting the first than the second point of view; ultimately it is a question of values.

APPENDIX
Sociology and Ethnosociology

Should there be only one science of human society and culture, or should there be at least two? This question assumes relevance when we ask what kind of relationship there is and ought to be between sociology and social anthropology, particularly in ex-colonial countries like India.

Each science must deal not only with the new realities it confronts as it advances, but also with the conceptual schemes and distinctions it inherits from the past. Students of society and culture in India, being latecomers in the field, find themselves in a somewhat delicate position. Should they devise their own conceptual categories out of their particular historical experience, ignoring the accumulated body of concepts built up within the discipline before they themselves entered the field? Or, should they take, as more or less finished products, the conceptual schemes and distinctions already available within their discipline, and apply them, even when they do less than full justice to their reality?

The distinction between sociology and social anthropology that we find in the Indian university system was not devised by Indian scholars themselves, but was acquired from the West. In the West itself this distinction became most marked in the period between the two world wars which was precisely the time when the sciences of society and culture were beginning to take root in India. If many Indian social scientists are perplexed by this distinction today, it is because it does not correspond to their conditions of work, which in any case was not the main source from which it grew.

In the United Kingdom the objective condition to which the distinction between sociology and social anthropology corresponded was the distinction between society and culture in the metropolitan country, and in the colonies, particularly the more backward areas of these colonies. In the United States it was the distinction between life in the industrial city and in the tribal reservation. No two worlds could be more sharply separated than the aggressive, expanding world of the American city and the stagnant, moribund world of the American reservation. Small wonder, therefore, that the distinction between sociology and social anthropology was more marked in the United States than in any other country. Again, it may not be an accident that in the United Kingdom the distinction between the two became less marked after the loss of empire which reduced the sharpness of the distinction between the metropolitan country and the colonies.

The period between the two wars was the period when students of society and culture in the United Kingdom and the United States began to concentrate on detailed empirical studies, whether through survey research or through participant-observation. The intense preoccupation with empirical research made the gulf wider between sociologists and social anthropologists in terms of the work they actually did. It made a lot of difference whether a man went off to study a tribe in darkest Africa or investigated the leisure-time activities of middle-class housewives in his own city. The difference was further accentuated by the fact that anthropologists tended to show a preference for the most primitive, and sociologists for the most advanced societies.

The objective conditions of work in India are very different, although the old labels are still put to use. Almost all Indians—whether 'sociologists' or 'social anthropologists'—study one or another sector of Indian society which is, on the whole, neither too primitive nor too advanced. When an Indian studies a 'tribal' village he is an 'anthropologist' and when he studies a 'non-tribal' village he is a 'sociologist'; or, when he studies a village, tribal or non-tribal, he is an 'anthropologist', but when he studies a town or city, he is a 'sociologist'. But the point is simply this, that the distinction between 'tribal' and 'non-tribal' village, or between village and town in India is of a totally different kind from the distinction between city and reservation in the United States, or between metropolitan country and colony in the British Empire.

It is true that few serious scholars in the United Kingdom or the United States would seek to justify today the distinction between social anthropology and sociology in terms of the distinction between primitive and advanced societies. Indeed, many would at least in principle be in favour of abandoning or at least ignoring the first distinction itself. But the objective conditions which gave rise to the distinction have not fully disappeared and the distinction itself has become firmly entrenched in the organization of the profession, so that it tends to reappear in new forms from time to time.

In the United States people talk increasingly of ethnosociology, which presumably is either distinct from sociology or a distinct branch of sociology, and some Indians are also beginning to follow this usage. Ethnosociology, put in very simple terms, is the study of society and culture through use of the native concepts and categories of the people being studied. In my view there is little more to the new distinction than there was to the old distinction between social anthropology and sociology. I find that in bilingual journals the word *ethnosociologue* is used in French to translate the English term 'social anthropologist'.

The United States is where one sees the most active interest in the 'ethnosciences' today. There was ethnomethodology, there is ethnosociology, and I understand that there is now ethnohistory. The choice of the prefix 'ethno' is unfortunate, for the term 'ethnic' is a little like the word 'native'. There is of course one sense in which everybody is a native, of one country or another; but there is another sense, which everybody understands, in which only some are natives and not others. So it is with ethnics or ethnic groups. In the United States, Italians, Irishmen, Jews, Poles, Greeks and others are ethnics; but white Anglo-Saxon Protestants are, by convention, not.

The British made a simple distinction between themselves and the natives; when they studied themselves they were sociologists, when they studied the natives they became social anthropologists. I think that there is a tendency for Americans to make a similar distinction, though not as explicitly. When they study the core of their own society and culture they are sociologists. When they study other societies and cultures, particularly in Africa, Asia and Latin America (or marginal groups in their own society), they tend to become ethnosociologists. The great pity is that some Indians are now inclined to feel that they ought to apply the same distinctions among themselves.

The plea that those who study society and culture through the concepts and categories of the people being studied are distinct from other sociologists, and should be called ethnosociologists, does not appear very convincing. By this kind of reasoning Talcott Parsons should be the most outstanding ethnosociologist in the United States for has he not used the concepts and categories of the American people themselves in trying to arrive at an understanding of American society and culture? Yet, to my knowledge, nobody has described Parsons as an ethnosociologist. I have failed to perceive a clear rationale in the distinction between sociology and ethnosociology. What is obvious, however, is that it is similar in structure to a distinction that is present in American society itself. Ethnic groups are people of other kinds; ethnosociology is the study of other societies and cultures through the use of native concepts and categories.

2
Peasant Studies and their Significance

THE STUDY OF peasant communities, or of peasantry in the broad sense, is of major interest to sociologists and social anthropologists today. In this sense their present field of interest is somewhat different from what it was a hundred years ago. Sociologists and social anthropologists started by studying complex industrial societies at one end and primitive tribal societies at the other. By moving into the field of peasant studies they are seeking to make their investigations into the nature and types of human society more comprehensive if not complete.

Students of human society discovered not only a new field of study, but one which called upon them to combine the traditional skills of social anthropology and of sociology. From the viewpoint of comparative sociology an interesting feature of peasants is that they have, on the one hand, an elaborate system of kinship and marriage, and are, on the other, part of a complex system of stratification and class.

As noted earlier, social anthropologists have from the very beginning paid special attention to the study of kinship systems. It is not as if they have not studied other institutional systems. But these studies they have from the very beginning shared to some extent with others, whereas kinship studies is the one area of investigation which they have made their very own. Sociology in the narrow sense paid little attention to the systematic study of the relations of kinship and marriage outside the limited sphere of the family system. The reason for this is not far to seek. The study of 'advanced' industrial societies does not call for detailed analysis of the relations of kinship and affinity, for in these societies the scope of such relations is greatly restricted. On the other hand, the study of 'primitive' tribal societies demands the analysis of the kinship system which often provides the basic design for these societies.

Now the kinship system, though not coterminous with the whole community, plays a very significant part in peasant social life. No analysis of it can be complete which does not go into the details of the differentiation of social roles according to the ties of blood and marriage. In India the student of peasant social organization, no matter what his area of special interest, must look into the structure of corporate groups like the lineage and the nature of interpersonal relations among agnates, cognates and affines. This is even more manifestly the case for pre-Communist China; the available studies of peasant communities in China do in fact give a prominent place to clan, lineage and kinship.

If the study of kinship and marriage gave to traditional anthropology its specific concerns, classical sociology acquired its distinctive character from the study of class and stratification. Once again, this is not to deny the other interests of sociologists but only to observe that what distinguished classical sociology from all other disciplines, and more particularly anthropology, was its preoccupation with the problems of inequality. It is not difficult to see why sociologists paid so much attention to class and stratification and why social anthropologists neglected them. Sociology became a discipline mainly through the study of Western industrial societies. These societies, which drew the interest of the vast majority of sociologists, were, unlike those studied by the anthropologists, characterized by the presence of groups and categories which were elaborately ranked and between which there were visible conflicts of interest. The sociologist could no more ignore class and stratification than the anthropologist could ignore kinship and marriage.

Peasant studies not only involve the analysis of kinship and marriage but also require an understanding of stratification and class. Firstly, peasants are internally subdivided in terms of income and size of holding into, let us say, poor, middle and rich peasants; in India they might, in addition, be divided into different castes. But what is more important is that they form only one stratum or class in a complex system of classes and strata; no understanding of the peasants can be complete unless we see them in relation to non-working landowners on the one hand and landless workers on the other.

The study of peasant communities by sociologists and social anthropologists is of fairly recent origin. The first full-length community studies began to be published just before the Second War, and it is only during the last two decades that they have acquired their present significance. Among social anthropologists in the West peasant studies are gradually coming to acquire the position enjoyed by tribal studies in the years before the War. Part of the interest of contemporary Western scholars in the peasantry is fed by the awareness of the growing importance of the Third World. India, China and the countries of Africa and Latin America were till the end of the War of interest mainly to historians and ethnographers, i.e. scholars who recorded unfamiliar customs from either the past or the present. But with the end of the colonial era these countries have assumed a much more immediate contemporary relevance in the world as a whole. Not unreasonably, many people in the West have begun to feel that the best way to understand them is to investigate the social, economic and political problems of their peasantry.

The study of peasant communities is also a part of the process of self-awareness in the Third World itself. Asian, African and Latin American countries are now no longer entirely dependent for sociological investigations on scholars from the advanced nations. They are now producing their own sociologists for whom the study of peasant communities is naturally becoming a major undertaking. This field has both a theoretical and a practical side. On the practical side it is intimately associated with programmes of development and modernization. The peasantry has been for centuries characterized as backward and conservative. Much of the economic backwardness and social conservatism of the countries of the Third World has for long been attributed to the innate characteristics of the peasantry. As these countries embark on programmes of development and modernization it becomes necessary to discover the most effective means of changing their conditions of life. In both China and India rural development programmes have played an important part in creating interest in the study of peasant communities.

In very recent times a somewhat different image of the peasantry has emerged in certain quarters. This is what one might describe as the revolutionary as opposed to the conservative image, where the true repository of revolutionary potential in the Third World is considered to be the peasantry; any major revolution here must be rooted in the social and political situation of the peasantry. For this reason the conditions of life of the peasantry, and peasant movements and associations are becoming important subjects of investigation in Asia and Latin America. Needless to say, these subjects become the concern of both enthusiasts of revolutionary change and experts in 'revolutionary prophylaxis'.

The field of peasant studies is rather vaguely defined. This is partly because the field itself is relatively new, and partly because the approaches to it are many and varied. Students of economic processes and of social institutions have somewhat different—though not necessarily contradictory—perspectives on the problem. The concept of 'peasant economy' developed by Chayanov and his school is being revived by some contemporary students of the peasantry.[1] A somewhat different orientation is to be found among the generality of social anthropologists whose interest is in the study of 'peasant society and culture'.

Corresponding to these differences in orientation there are differences in the use of concepts. Even among sociologists and social anthropologists there is no general agreement about the meanings attached to such terms as 'peasantry', 'peasant community' and 'peasant society'.[2] Anthropologists are sometimes inclined to use 'peasant society' as a residual category, putting together all kinds of societies which are neither clearly 'tribal' nor clearly 'industrial'. This is a source of confusion because, while peasants might share certain common characteristics throughout the world, the so-called peasant societies differ very much from each other. These questions will have to be discussed in Chapter 3. Perhaps it will be better for the time being to consider agrarian rather than peasant societies, and to discuss peasant communities wherever these are found within this broad category of societies.

Despite their many limitations and ambiguities, studies of peasant communities have come to stay in sociology and social anthropology. Indeed, in Asian countries it is to these studies that the science of society owes much of its present shape. By basing themselves on the study of the peasantry, students of social life in these countries can

---

[1] See, for instance, A. V. Chayanov, *The Theory of Peasant Economy*, edited by Daniel Thorner, B. Kerblay and R. E. F. Smith, Irwin, 1966.

[2] For a recent discussion see Teodor Shanin (ed.), *Peasants and Peasant Societies*, Penguin, 1971, particularly the Introduction.

by-pass the distinction between sociology and social anthropology which has bedevilled Western scholars for generations.

A sufficiently large number of studies of peasant communities from all over the world are now available to make some kind of stock-taking a worthwhile exercise. We shall begin with a consideration of the circumstances under which peasant studies by sociologists and social anthropologists came into being. We shall then discuss some of the major findings of these studies, particularly from the Asian countries. A great deal can be learned by comparing the Indian with the Chinese studies made in the field. We shall conclude with a brief discussion of similar studies of European peasant communities.

Several intellectual streams have contributed to the present interest among social anthropologists in the study of peasant communities. From the viewpoint of the discipline, the work of Redfield and his associates occupies a unique position. Redfield not only gave a new direction to anthropology in the United States, but also influenced significantly the work of scholars in Latin America, India and to some extent also China. British anthropologists held out against the new wave for some time, but the study of peasant communities has come to occupy an increasingly important place in their work in recent times.

Redfield's book on Tepoztlan[3] was the first full-length study of a peasant community using modern anthropological techniques of research. In the thirties Redfield made further empirical studies of Mexican communities and set a new trend of research among his American colleagues. It did not take anthropologists long to realize that a vast new field was lying unexplored, and Redfield turned their attention to it at a particularly opportune moment, when the possibilities of tribal studies within the United States were becoming more and more exhausted.

The work of Redfield and his colleagues helped to create a new image of anthropology. Anthropology could no longer be described as 'the investigation of oddments by the eccentric'.[4] It is true that the work of Malinowski and his associates had paved the way for a more realistic and down-to-earth appraisal of tribal societies. But these

[3] Robert Redfield, *Tepoztlan, a Mexican Village: A Study of Folk Life*, University of Chicago Press, 1930.

[4] Clyde Kluckhohn, cited in Max Gluckman, *Politics, Law and Ritual in Tribal Societies*, Basil Blackwell, 1965.

societies were still too remote and far away to have much more than an exotic appeal to the intelligentsia in America, Europe or even Asia. The study of peasant communities brought anthropology to the doorstep of all students of society and culture in the Third World.

The study of peasant communities not only gave anthropology access to a substantial section of the world's population, but it also opened up a new approach to the understanding of civilizations. Field investigations and literary studies had become distinct and separate activities. The anthropologist studied tribal communities in the field; these communities were isolated, self-sufficient and devoid of any written records about their past. The historian and classicist studied civilizations by examinining literary sources handed down from the past. Peasant communities required to be investigated in the field; but they were also parts of a larger civilization which had to be understood in order to make the investigation complete.

Redfield's own work in Mexico assembled a wealth of new empirical material. It revealed in simple, non-technical language the nature of peasant social structure and its links with the outside world. It also presented a vivid picture of the beliefs, values and attitudes of the Mexican peasant. The great merit of Redfield's empirical work was that it brought together material from tribal, peasant and urban communities.[5] By doing this he was able to link the study of peasant communities with the traditional concerns of social anthropology and sociology.

Redfield presented his empirical material in an attractive theoretical framework. The conception of a 'folk-urban continuum' enabled him to see Mexican society as a whole by examining it closely at certain crucial points. The remote tribal community, the peasant village, the small town and the larger urban centre bore a family resemblance to each other; but they represented different degrees of structural and cultural complexity.[6] The anthropologist was being offered at one and the same time a method for the study of peasant communities and a typology of various communities. In constructing this typology Redfield drew heavily on the work of nineteenth century sociologists such as Tönnies, Durkheim and Maine.

Redfield devoted his later writings to discussions of the little community in general and the peasant community in particular. His characterization of the social, cultural and psychological attributes of the peasantry has become justly famous. In the last book he

[5] In particular *The Folk Culture of Yucatan*, University of Chicago Press, 1941.
[6] Ibid.

wrote, *Peasant Society and Culture*,[7] he surveyed the empirical material on the peasantry brought together by anthropologists during the two preceding decades and on this basis tried to formulate the common characteristics of peasants throughout the world. Following Kroeber, Redfield defined peasants as being part-societies and part-cultures.[8] This is the characteristic anthropological definition which, viewing peasants in opposition to tribals, emphasizes their articulation with the wider society and culture. Economists, on the other hand, tend to view peasants in opposition to farmers, emphasizing their isolation from the wider market economy. Needless to say, there are several contemporary anthropologists who give a prominent place to isolation from the market in characterizing the peasantry.[9]

The work of Redfield and his associates underlined the organic character of the peasant community. Peasant social life is seen as being governed by certain common social values emphasizing the virtues of work, the obligations to kin and neighbours, and reverence for the supernatural. The peasant community is small and homogeneous, and the relations between its members have a direct and personal quality. The even tenor of peasant social life is not normally disturbed by the kinds of conflict and violence which are common features of urban industrial life. There is evidently a family resemblance between Redfield's picture of the peasant community and Tönnies's model of Gemeinschaft.

Other observers of peasant communities have found these conceptions idealized and perhaps slightly romantic. Closer analyses show such communities to be often sharply divided by conflicting interests.[10] Perhaps the limitation lay not so much in Redfield's empirical investigations as in his conceptual framework. When one seeks to understand peasant communities primarily in terms of a set of common values there is a tendency to represent them as harmonious. A more realistic representation must pay adequate attention to the material basis of peasant social life.[11]

The field that was opened up by Redfield with his Mexican

[7] Robert Redfield, *Peasant Society and Culture, An Anthropological Approach to Civilization*, University of Chicago Press, 1956.   [8] Ibid.

[9] See, for instance, Eric Wolf, *Peasants*, Prentice-Hall, 1966.

[10] See, for instance, the restudy of Tepoztlan by Oscar Lewis in which a contrasting picture of the same village is presented. Oscar Lewis, *Life in a Mexican Village: Tepoztlan Restudied*, University of Illinois Press, 1951.

[11] André Béteille, 'Ideas and Interests: Some Conceptual Problems in the Study of Social Stratification in Rural India', *International Social Science Journal*, Vol. XXI, No. 2, 1969, pp. 219–34.

studies was soon extended into the Old World. After all, it is the principal Asian countries that have the largest number of peasant communities and have had them for the longest time. The Latin American peasantry by contrast is of relatively recent origin, and it has emerged under somewhat special conditions. In India and China peasant communities have existed in their natural condition for millennia. It is here that the study of peasant communities holds the promise of a living understanding of the world's most ancient civilizations.

There were other reasons behind the rapid growth of Western interest in the peasant communities of Asia. American social scientists have always been characterized by a practical approach to problems. They must have realized very quickly that in the post-colonial era Asia would become a major field of foreign policy interest in their own country. Consequently, the study of peasant society and culture in these countries was likely to receive vast governmental patronage. This of course is not to say that American social scientists working in the Third World have always allowed themselves to be used as instruments of American foreign policy.

Redfield himself was closely though indirectly associated with the study of peasantry in both China and India. Fei Hsiao-Tung was invited to the University of Chicago where, with the assistance of Mrs Redfield, he prepared his book on the Chinese gentry,[12] which was in a way complementary to his earlier work on peasant life in China. Redfield's influence on community studies in India made by both American and Indian scholars is well known; it was largely under his influence (and that of Milton Singer) that the studies brought together in *Village India* came into being.

But there were other sources of inspiration for peasant studies in Asia. It would be fair to say that the inter-War period was the time when Asian scholars began to take an active interest in their own peasantry, and some of them found the new anthropology a useful instrument which they sought to adapt to their own purpose. This was certainly the context in which anthropology was introduced into China, and this context has to be kept in mind if we are to understand the shape taken by the subject in India.

Countries like India and China have had an indigenous intelligentsia for centuries. Towards the end of the colonial era this

---

[12] Fei Hsiao-Tung, *China's Gentry*, University of Chicago Press, 1953.

intelligentsia, which was highly urbanized, found itself in a general way cut off from its own social and cultural roots. This was the time when a growing awareness emerged that the real Asia was the Asia of the villages. In India this awareness was most clearly articulated by Tagore and Gandhi, both of whom influenced the work of the anthropologist N. K. Bose. Bose sought to use his anthropological training to investigate problems which were brought to the surface by the nationalist movement;[13] outside anthropology there were of course other social scientists who were engaged in a similar venture.

As for China, Fei Hsiao-Tung describes how scholars like himself reacted against the inadequacies of traditional scholarship,[14] which was essentially literary and placed a kind of final value on the wisdom contained in the books. It served its purpose so long as the world was relatively unchanging and people more or less accepted the existing order of things. But in China, as in India, the vast social and economic changes of the twentieth century turned the attention of the scholars to peasants in the villages, and it was here that they found the traditional methods of scholarship inadequate. To understand peasant social life by living among the peasants through direct and systematic observation was something new which Western social science contributed to China.

The aims of Fei and his colleagues were largely those of social reconstruction. Their complaint against the traditional scholarship was that it provided very little guidance for practical action in a changing environment. They saw the problem of China as being rooted in the poverty, unemployment and exploitation of the peasantry. They were concerned about the disintegration of the traditional social order which had given the peasants some measure of security and well-being. They felt that the urgent task of social reconstruction called for the application of scientific methods to the understanding of social and economic processes. It was in this context that sociology and social anthropology began to take roots in pre-Communist China.

In India the relationship between social reconstruction and sociological investigation has been more complex. While centres such as Tagore's Sriniketan tried from the beginning to combine the two, the university departments in general took a more academic view of

[13] N. K. Bose, *Culture and Society in India*, Asia, 1967.
[14] Fei Hsiao-Tung and Chang Chih-I, *Earthbound China, A Study of Rural Economy in Yunnan*, Routledge and Kegan Paul, 1949.

the problem. Further, social scientists in India were perhaps concerned to a greater extent than their Chinese colleagues with the demands of their discipline so that we see in their work a more active and continuous preoccupation with concepts, methods and theories considered independently of social action.

The studies made in the thirties and forties by Chinese sociologists of peasant communities in China deserve attention for a variety of reasons. In spite of the very different paths taken by India and China since 1947, the two countries have a common background and a common set of social, economic and political problems which become particularly clear when we consider the situation of the peasantry. The similarities between the Chinese and the Indian peasantry are no less striking than their differences. Indian sociologists tend to ignore the fact that several village studies were made by Chinese sociologists and published during the decade before the Communist régime was established. A comparison of Chinese and Indian village studies will also provide an interesting exercise in the sociology of knowledge. The impact of Western ideas, including Western social science, was very different in the two countries. Chinese scholars took to village studies after a very brief exposure to Western sociology, whereas in India these studies came to be made after a relatively long acquaintance with British and American sociology and social anthropology. What differences do we find in the concepts, methods and theories applied to village studies in the two countries?

The first full-length study of a Chinese village was published in 1939 by Fei Hsiao-Tung.[15] This work was completed under the supervision of Malinowski at the London School of Economics and it carries a Foreword by him. In a later work[16] Fei has acknowledged his intellectual debt to two other scholars, Robert Park, the American sociologist and S. M. Shirokogoroff, the Russian ethnologist. These intellectual influences were used with discrimination and in the work itself there is no attempt to enter into the controversies then prevalent in Western sociology.

Fei's description of his village is presented in a matter-of-fact way without any effort to enter into conceptual or theoretical niceties. The principal objective was to observe carefully and record faithfully

[15] Fei Hsiao-Tung, *Peasant Life in China*, Routledge and Kegan Paul, 1939.
[16] Fei Hsiao-Tung, 'Introduction' in Fei and Chang, *Earthbound China*, op. cit.

the different aspects of the social life of the community. One notices two features of the framework of analysis which Malinowski had successfully established among his associates. The first was to show the social and cultural activities of the peasants in their manifold interrelatedness. The second was to concentrate on the day-to-day life of the people rather than on the colourful and the spectacular. Kiangts'un, the village studied by Fei, is described in terms of the cycle of work or economic activities, domestic life and the kinship system, and ceremonial life or the cycle of rituals. There is a close interdependence between the three in Kiangts'un as in most peasant communities. The unit of economic activities on the peasant farm is the peasant household, and most of the important ceremonies are connected with either the cycle of economic activities or the domestic cycle of birth, marriage and death.

A second full-length study of a different part of China was published shortly afterwards: the account by Martin Yang of Taitou, the village in which he himself grew up in Shantung province.[17] Unlike Kiangts'un, which was a rice-growing village, Taitou was located in the wheat-growing region, and consequently there were differences between the two in their patterns of agriculture. However, both villages were characterized by small holdings, and were in this way basically similar in their productive systems, although the inhabitants of Taitou depended solely on agriculture whereas those of Kiangts'un combined agriculture with village industry.

Taitou was a village of small peasants. Yang divided its population into four categories according to the amount of land held, and the wealthiest families owned under ten acres each. Almost all adults, both men and women, worked in the fields, although those who were wealthy tended to withdraw from the heavier work as they advanced in years. The village did not have a very elaborate division of labour. There were only a few families of artisans. Blacksmiths, carpenters, weavers, oil-pressers and masons did not constitute specialized groups but were drawn from among the peasants themselves. Yang discusses the peasant community in terms of the structure of its basic groups and categories. He views social groups as being of different kinds, and takes the family which is the 'most primary group' as his point of departure. The village, unlike the family, is in his view a secondary group. He shows how the family is

[17] Martin Yang, *A Chinese Village: Taitou, Shantung Province*, Routledge and Kegan Paul, 1948.

structurally linked to the village through various 'transitional groups' such as clans, neighbourhoods and other socio-economic and socio-religious groups. Finally he shows how the village is linked with the market town and with other villages served by the same market town.

In some ways the most characteristic among the studies of Chinese peasant communities is the set of three studies made by Fei Hsiao-Tung and Chang Chih-I and brought together in *Earthbound China*.[18] These three villages were selected, along with the one described in *Peasant Life in China*, to represent different types of productive arrangements, and their comparative study gives valuable insights into the broader economic forces at work in the Chinese countryside. It is unfortunate that the larger project of which these studies were a part, and whose design is briefly explained in Fei's Introduction to *Earthbound China*, had to remain incomplete.

Earthbound China is an attempt to explore systematically the institutional background of the Chinese rural economy. Fei relates the study of the three village communities to the earlier work of Tawney and of Buck. Certain important questions are raised on methodology, and, in particular, on how far it is possible to understand the social and economic organization of the Chinese farm through the methods of survey research. Fei has no difficulty in showing that Buck, who based his own important work on survey research, was misled on a number of fundamental points. In particular, he criticizes Buck for trying to understand the Chinese rural economy in terms of the 'conventional American classification into owners, part-owners and tenants'.[19] Tenancy in China meant something quite different from tenancy in America; and in China itself tenants of clan land and of individual land had very different obligations. An understanding of these important factors required intensive investigation by the methods of participant-observation. Students of the Indian village community will find familiar questions being raised here on the relative advantages of different methods of investigation.

In regard to typology, Fei urges caution over the use of generalized and abstract cultural categories. He maintains, quite reasonably, that the typology must reflect the basic interests of the investigation.

---

[18] Fei and Chang, *Earthbound China*, op. cit. Interestingly, Fei tells us that the title of the book was suggested by Malinowski before it was actually written.

[19] Ibid., p. 2.

The basic interests in this study are in poverty, landlessness, inefficient technology and the exploitation of the country by the town. The typology presented here is by no means exhaustive, for all the three villages are located in the same ecological region, far away from the centres of Chinese civilization. The book nevertheless provides a valuable introduction to an understanding of the economic and social problems of rural China.

All three Yunnan villages were characterized by small or dwarf holdings rarely exceeding ten acres. In all three most adult members of both sexes participated in some form of agricultural work. The division of labour between agriculture and handicraft was not very rigidly maintained. Individuals often combined a variety of occupational roles, either at the same time or at different stages in their life. There were also differences between the three communities. In the first village, Luts'un, most of the landowners were resident and their holdings were uniformly small. In the second village, Yits'un, there were several relatively large landowners possessing land in other villages, while others were small occupying owners; however, the land owned outside the village was often poor in quality and the returns from it were uncertain. The third community, Yuts'un, had many tenants while its big landowners lived outside in nearby towns. These three villages are compared with Kiangts'un, a community of tenants whose absentee landlords lived in large towns, this being described as 'a further development of tenancy than in the third type'.[20] The economic problems in the three Yunnan villages are discussed in the context of their social framework. The main emphasis in the discussion is naturally on the organization of work and the part played in it by the different categories of villagers. The family emerges once again as the primary unit of both production and consumption. The study concludes with a discussion of the best way of combining agriculture with rural industry so as to ensure viability for the farm family.

The work begun by Fei and his colleagues at the National Yunnan University had to be discontinued before the Communists came to power. There is little authentic sociological data on Chinese peasant communities after 1949. C. K. Yang's study of Nanching, a village on the fringe of Canton city, gives some idea of a peasant community during the transition from the old to the new social order.[21] This

---

[20] Ibid., p. 17.
[21] C. K. Yang, *A Chinese Village in Early Communist Transition*, Harvard University Press, 1959.

study once again emphasizes the distribution of land and the organization of production, and discusses the changes brought about in both during the first phase of land reforms. Thus, the village studies from China were not only all conducted within a brief period of time, but are all characterized by a certain unity of approach and a concern for certain common problems, those centring around the ownership, control and use of land.

Whereas in China village studies by sociologists virtually came to an end around 1949, in India it was only after Independence in 1947 that they were begun in a really serious way. Although India has had a longer and more continuous tradition of social science research, the first full-length sociological study of an Indian village was published as late as 1955, a decade and a half after the publication of Fei's book on Kiangts'un. Indian sociologists turned to the study of peasant communities after the discipline had become established in the country; for this reason we find a somewhat greater theoretical sophistication in their work than in the Chinese village studies.

Although Chinese and Indian village communities share many features in common, the emphases in the two sets of studies are somewhat different. The Chinese studies, as we have noted, focus the attention on the peasant and his farm, and on the social and economic consequences of fragmented holdings, tenancy and landlessness. These problems have until recently played a less important part in the studies made by sociologists and social anthropologists of Indian village communities. Part of this is no doubt due to the fact that in India a division of labour between economists and sociologists had already become established when village studies were begun by the latter.

We have, of course, a much more comprehensive picture of village communities in India than we have for China. We not only have studies covering almost all the major regions of India but these studies deal with almost every aspect of institutional life. An important reason for the variety of these studies is that they have been made by sociologists and social anthropologists not only from India but from all over the world.

The first full-length sociological study of an Indian village, by S. C. Dube, was published in 1955.[22] He had been trained as an

---

[22] S. C. Dube, *Indian Village*, Routledge and Kegan Paul, 1955.

anthropologist and earlier made a study of a small tribal group with a simple technology.[23] Dube's study of the village Shamirpet gave a clear indication of the new direction of research in Indian sociology. He emphasized the need, first, to understand the internal heterogeneity of the non-tribal village, and, second, to examine it in its manifold relationship with the outside world.

We should remember that the first full-length study of an Indian village was the outcome of a very practical programme, viz. the Osmania University Social Service Extension Project. The study also benefited from and was to a certain extent shaped by the fact that the project was interdisciplinary in character. There were economists, agronomists and experts on health and nutrition in the team, whose work was done under the general supervision of Dube. Dube pursued his interest in the study of extension programmes by publishing a few years later a book on the social and cultural implications of the Community Development Programme.[24]

Dube's book on Shamirpet is in the style of the old anthropological monographs. It does not seek to focus attention on any particular problem or institutional system, but provides a general and comprehensive account of all the major areas of village life. There is first an account of the major social categories in the village in terms of religion and caste. Then there are descriptions of the economic system, the ritual system and the family system. The book concludes with a discussion of the changes coming about in the Indian village. We clearly get the impression that Dube's village is more complex and more highly stratified than the peasant communities studied by Fei.

An important landmark in the development of village studies in India was the publication in 1955 of a collection of eight essays edited by Marriott,[25] which provides descriptive accounts of villages in different parts of India. But more important than that, it raises fundamental questions of methodology. To what extent can the Indian village be treated as a social and cultural isolate? Given the fact that it is not wholly isolated, what kind of strategy should the anthropologist adopt in order to provide a meaningful account of it? The book was clearly designed to answer questions whose roots lay in the intellectual discipline of anthropology.

The studies brought together in *Village India* not only raised

[23] S. C. Dube, *The Kamar*, Universal Publishers, 1951.
[24] S. C. Dube, *India's Changing Villages*, Routledge and Kegan Paul, 1958.
[25] McKim Marriott (ed.). *Village India*, University of Chicago Press, 1955.

important questions of methodology but also generated a number of valuable concepts. In his essay on Rampura Srinivas put forward the important concept of the dominant caste which was to figure prominently in later writings on the Indian village. Marriott in his essay on Kishan Garhi formulated the two related concepts of 'universalization' and 'parochialization' with a view to interpreting the active relationship between the great and the little traditions.

The relatively high level of sophistication of the anthropologists who were studying rural India generated some technical and abstruse controversies such as that concerning the sociological reality of the Indian village. In a provocative article Dumont and Pocock wrote that the real problems of sociological analysis in India should centre around kinship, caste and religion, and that the Indian village lacked sociological reality;[26] Bailey wrote an effective rejoinder, defending the validity of taking the village as the basic unit of investigation.[27] Their relative lack of sophistication had protected the Chinese anthropolgists from debates of this kind.

The eight essays brought together in *Village India* reveal clearly the structural diversity of village communities in the country. There are villages like Rampura in Mysore state which can be properly described as peasant communities. Here most of the land is owned by the Okkaligas who are a cultivating caste and constitute about half the population of the village. Most of the land is in small and medium holdings, and much of the production is organized on the basis of family labour with some use of hired labour for particular operations and on particular occasions. In contrast to Rampura is the village of Kumbapettai, described by Kathleen Gough, where the Brahmins constitute the dominant caste. Villages of the type of Kumbapettai—by no means rare in Tanjore or in India as a whole—have not only a more elaborate caste hierarchy but also a more complex structure of agrarian relations. Where Brahmins own most of the land, production is organized not on the basis of family labour but on the basis of either tenancy or wage labour. It is doubtful if villages like Kumbapettai can be properly described as peasant communities, for the Brahmins who constitute the dominant group in such villages can hardly be characterized as peasants.

[26] Louis Dumont and David F. Pocock, 'Village Studies', *Contributions to Indian Sociology*, No. 1, 1957.

[27] F. G. Bailey, 'For a Sociology of India?' *Contributions to Indian Sociology*, No. 3, 1959, pp. 88–101.

Village India (and its companion volume, *India's Villages*, published in the same year)[28] was followed by a succession of monographs on individual villages from different parts of the country. These monographs tended to focus attention on particular aspects of village social structure. Thus some emphasized economic processes, others dwelt on kinship and yet others concentrated on ritual. But all of them gave a special place to the caste structure of the village as providing the basic framework of analysis.[29] In fact, the study of village social structure and of caste at the village level became almost synonymous, the village providing a convenient physical locus for the study of intercaste relations on the ground.

This overemphasis on caste among students of the Indian village led them to neglect one of the most crucial features of a peasant social and economic system, the technical and social organization of production. Because of the overwhelming influence of Redfield many of them characterized their work, rather vaguely, as the study of peasant communities. Yet if they had examined a little more closely the productive systems of the villages they were studying, they would have seen that these were not all communities of peasants, but were often divided into landlords, tenants and landless labourers.

An attempt had in fact been made nearly thirty years ago by Ramkrishna Mukherjee to study villages in the Indian subcontinent in terms of their productive organization.[30] And Mukherjee had begun by raising the question as to whether these could be regarded as communities of peasants. His aim was to marshal statistical evidence which would challenge the widely-prevalent myth of the egalitarian Indian village. Mukherjee's work was done before the partition of India, in the Bogra district of what is now Bangladesh. There was a long gap between his fieldwork and the publication of his material in book form. The published material itself has been presented in terms of highly formal categories, and we do not get from it the same insight into the working of village social life that we get from the Chinese monographs or from the later Indian monographs. For these and other reasons Mukherjee's studies did not make a substantial impact on the work taken up by the next

[28] M. N. Srinivas (ed.), *India's Villages*, Asia, 1960.
[29] Béteille, 'Ideas and Interests', op. cit.
[30] Ramkrishna Mukherjee, *Six Villages of Bengal*, Popular Prakashan, 1971; also *The Dynamics of a Rural Society*, Akademie Verlag, 1957.

generation of sociologists and social anthropologists in rural India.

It is now almost twenty years since the first studies of the Indian village using caste as the basic frame of reference began to be published. During this period almost every aspect of caste as it operates at the village level has been explored. There are signs that the new generation of sociologists would like to turn from caste to the study of the relations centring around the ownership, control and use of land. It might be worth their while at this juncture to look at the work which had been done with so much patience and care—and under such difficult conditions—by their predecessors in China.

Peasant communities are found not only in Asia, Africa and Latin America, but also in most of the European countries. The peasantry did not attract much attention from the founders of European sociology with a few exceptions; they were believed to be a declining force in the face of the newly-emerging industrial social order. However, in several East European countries the peasants constitute a substantial section of the population even today. In countries like Italy, France and Austria also, the peasant question is an important one both economically and politically.[31]

The 'peasant question' has of course held the attention of European scholars for several generations, but in Western Europe in particular it has been a question more in the realm of economic history than of sociology or anthropology. The issues in the study of the European peasantry were either economic, centring around inadequate technology, low productivity and declining consumption; or political, centring around peasant conservatism and the role of the peasant lobby in national politics. The techniques developed by Redfield for understanding a civilization through the study of peasant communities were rarely applied in the European countries. Hence we know much about the economic and political problems of the European peasantry but less about their social and cultural characteristics.

We now have a few full-length studies by social anthropologists of European peasant communities. One of the first was a study made by an American anthropologist, Joel Halpern, of a Serbian village

[31] For a useful recent discussion see S. H. Franklin, *The European Peasantry, The Final Phase*, Methuen, 1969.

in Yugoslavia.[32] Orasac, the village described by Halpern, is a typical peasant community in which the family farm is the centre of social and economic life. Unlike the case in many Indian villages, land is fairly equitably distributed so that there are no large landowners and few landless agricultural labourers. Those who own land cultivate it generally by their own labour and the labour of their family members; those who own no land generally work for wages outside agriculture.

This picture of a relatively homogeneous community of people with small family holdings on which both men and women work is confirmed by other available studies of peasant villages in both East and West Europe.[33] A recent study of a Hungarian village, Atany, by two Hungarian anthropologists, examines in detail work, leisure and family life among what the authors describe as 'proper peasants'.[34] Here also the family farm, on which both men and women do the work, constitutes the basic unit of social and economic life in the village.

It is not as if Orasac and Atany, any more than other peasant villages whether in East or West Europe, are fully egalitarian communities. There are rich and poor, landowning and landless people among them. But these are differences of degree rather than of kind. For all those who live on the land do much the same kind of work, and there is no unbridgeable gulf separating the rich landowners from the landless poor. It is only where the landowners become a permanent, self-perpetuating, non-working stratum and the landless are virtually cut off from all means of ownership or control of the land that we approach the negation of a peasant community.

[32] Joel M. Halpern, *A Serbian Village*, Columbia University Press, 1958.
[33] For West Europe see F. G. Bailey (ed.), *Gifts and Poison: The Politics of Reputation*, Basil Blackwell, 1971.
[34] Edit Fel and Tamas Hofer, *Proper Peasants: Traditional Life in a Hungarian Village*, Aldine Publishing Co., 1969.

3
The Concept of Peasant Society

THE DISCOVERY of the peasantry as a vast new field of investigation gave a dramatic turn to the development of sociology and social anthropology towards the middle of the present century. Social anthropology in particular acquired a new lease of life in the United States and Britain through studies of peasant communities in different parts of the world. If the primitive tribes had disappeared or were in the process of disappearing, there was a virtually inexhaustible supply of peasant communities in Asia, Latin America, Africa and even Europe.

It must be remembered that the anthropological understanding of the peasantry was achieved mainly through community studies. It was natural for students of these peasant communities to feel, as pioneers, that they were discovering—or at least exploring—a new kind of society of which the communities they studied were the building-blocks. Perhaps it was also natural on their part to claim that peasant societies predominated in almost every major region in the world. In this way countries as different as India and Ethiopia or Brazil and Yugoslavia came to be included in that vast and amorphous sociological category, the peasant society.

Now I am going to argue that it is one thing to talk about peasant communities in India (or China) and another to characterize Indian (or Chinese) society as a whole as a peasant society. There are peasant communities in both India and Yugoslavia, and a comparison of these will tell us something about the nature and types of communities. But it would be misleading to use this comparison as a basis for making statements about similarities and differences between Indian and Yugoslav societies.

The so-called peasant societies are sometimes very complex and highly stratified. They frequently include groups, classes and categories which cannot in any acceptable sense be regarded as peasants. Even where peasants are numerically preponderant the non-peasant strata may play a significant, or even decisive, part in the society taken as a whole. Further, the nature and role of these non-peasant strata may differ greatly from one society to another. Consequently, what are called peasant societies might share very little in common apart from the organizational features of one particular type of community.

Leaving aside altogether the contrast between urban and rural communities, it should be clear that in countries like India not all rural communities are communities of peasants. Indian villages, as we have seen, differ greatly in their structural type. There are some like Kumbapettai in which an elaborate hierarchy of caste is matched by an elaborate agrarian hierarchy. There are others like Rampura whose inhabitants are mainly smallholders belonging to the middle-level castes and who themselves cultivate the land. By applying the blanket term 'peasant community' to all of these we obscure significant differences in the types of agrarian structure in rural India.

The idea that village India is the physical locus of a peasant society seems to be the tacit assumption of a large number of sociologists and social anthropologists working in the Indian field. It is difficult to say how far Redfield himself would subscribe to this idea, but it is very much in evidence in the work of his followers both in India and abroad. While it may be useful to characterize some societies as peasant societies, it is doubtful whether one could properly do this in the case of traditional India with its elaborate caste hierarchy on the one hand and its complex agrarian stratification on the other.

The conceptual scheme which I would like to submit to critical examination can be seen in the form in which academic seminars on Indian society are often organized. It is common for such seminars to be divided into three sections, dealing with Urban Society, Peasant Society and Tribal Society. One can see at once the logic behind the scheme. Indian society is divided first into an urban and a rural sector. The rural sector is then divided into a tribal and a non-tribal sector. The non-tribal villages make up the peasant sector of Indian society.

Unfortunately, this rather facile scheme tends to be followed in the teaching of social anthropology in various universities. Students are taught something about urban India and tribal India, and then the rest of rural India is treated as if it constituted a society of peasants. This leaves them without any clear idea about the elaborate agrarian hierarchy which prevailed in traditional India and persists in many parts of the country even now. Further, some of the village studies through which 'peasant society' in India is illustrated are not studies of peasants alone, but of very heterogeneous communities.

One can see the shadow of Redfield's conceptual scheme in the division of Indian society into urban, peasant and tribal, but there is something basically unsatisfactory in the scheme as applied to India. Firstly, 'peasant society' as conceived in it is a residual category, and it has all the disadvantages of any residual category. It is conceived not in terms of any positive attributes, but as that sector of rural India which remains after the exclusion of tribal society. Part of this is due to the way in which sociology and social anthropology have developed in the West. We have seen that initially the former was concerned with industrial or urban and the latter with primitive or tribal societies. The middle ground, which had hitherto remained uncovered, was willy-nilly given the name of peasant society.

Secondly, while the non-tribal village is often too highly stratified to merit the name of peasant community, many of the so-called tribal villages in India are in fact communities of peasants. If we leave aside the small, nomadic hunting and gathering tribes, we will find that many of the larger tribes that live by settled agriculture are organized into communities which correspond very well to the classic conception of peasantry. I would go even further and argue that if one is looking for peasant communities in India the best place to begin would be among the Santals, the Oraons and the Mundas. In fact what I am suggesting is that we not only take a more critical look at our concept of peasant society but that we also thoroughly re-examine the tribe-peasant distinction around which much of our anthropological discussion seems to centre.

It should be emphasized that the issues involved are not merely terminological but substantive. It is not as if a particular sector of Indian society has been wrongly labelled as 'peasant society', and by giving it a different and more appropriate label our problem will be solved. I am also far from suggesting that the label 'peasant society' should now be attached to what we have been describing as 'tribal society' while a new label is thought out for the remainder of rural society.

My purpose is not to obscure the very real differences that exist among rural communities in India but to throw light on their true nature. The roots of these differences lie in a variety of factors among which the most important appear to be the distribution of land, the tenurial system, the structure of caste and the organization of work, including its division between men and women. An analysis of these will give a much deeper understanding of the varieties of rural communities in India than the use of blanket categories like 'peasant society' and 'tribal society'.

What should we mean by 'peasants' or 'peasantry'? *Chamber's Twentieth Century Dictionary* describes a peasant as 'a countryman: a rustic: one whose occupation is rural labour', and peasantry as 'the body of peasants or tillers of the soil: rustics: labourers'. In the English language—and also in other European languages—there appears to be an association between village life and a life of labour. In pre-industrial Europe gentlefolk lived not in villages but in manors, towns and cities. It would be dangerous to assume the validity of this kind of association for every society and culture. The *Shorter Oxford English Dictionary* defines a peasant as 'one who lives in the country and works on the land; a countryman, a rustic'. It adds in parentheses that in early use it referred properly only to people of foreign countries, 'often connoting the lowest rank, antithetical to *noble*'. It certainly had a derogatory connotation in Elizabethan English—'Oh what a rogue and peasant slave am I'— which it seems to retain in part even now. *Webster's Third New International Dictionary* describes the peasant as being of a class 'that tills the soil as small free landowners or hired labourers'. Webster points out that peasants are chiefly an European class, presumably with a view to underlining the contrast between Europe and North America. An additional meaning is given of the peasant as being 'a rather uneducated uncouth person in the low income group'.

In ordinary usage the term peasant has several closely related connotations among which I would now like to identify three. Firstly, the peasant is attached to the land. He not only lives on the land but by his labour makes the land bear fruit. The legal relation of the peasant to the land might vary. He might be an owner, a tenant or, in the limiting case, a labourer without any right of ownership or occupancy; but in all cases he earns his livelihood by labour. Within this framework one might give a broader or narrower connotation to the term. Some would limit it to owner-cultivators while others would include tenants and landless labourers as well.[1] Again, some would restrict it to tillers of the land while others would include in addition all those who live by the various forms of labour which are associated with a community of tillers.[2]

Secondly, peasants are viewed as occupying a low position in most societies. Even those who profess to admire the peasant qualities of hard work, thrift and simplicity concede that their actual rank in society is not high. The peasantry are often defined by opposition with the nobility or the gentry. 'Nobility' and 'gentry' are both terms with diverse meanings which need not be discussed here; we shall use the term 'gentry' in a very broad sense to refer to strata which live off the land but without engaging in labour. The contrast between peasantry and gentry must always be kept in mind, particularly when dealing with societies which are highly stratified.

The position of the peasantry in the order of stratification is viewed not simply in economic but also in cultural terms. Even when they own the land which they till, the holding is of small or medium size and the income from it barely sufficient to keep the family on the level of subsistence. But in addition to this, peasants are also viewed as 'rustics', i.e. persons who are untutored and unlettered. It is only the anthropologist who investigates peasant styles of life and peasant culture. In the popular meaning—which equates culture with refinement—the peasant lacks both style and culture.

The third shade of meaning derives from the language of political debate. Just as in one sense peasantry are the opposite of gentry, so also in another are peasants the counterparts of workers. The slogan 'peasants and workers' has a familiar ring in all Asian countries. This slogan draws attention to the oppression and exploitation suffered by the peasants at the hands of various classes. It

---

[1] See Daniel Thorner, 'Peasantry' in David L. Sils (ed.), *International Encyclopedia of the Social Sciences*, The Macmillan Company & The Free Press, 1968, Vol. 11, pp. 503–11.

[2] Raymond Firth seems to prefer this broader conception; see his *Malay Fishermen, Their Peasant Economy*, Routledge and Kegan Paul, 1946.

assumes a clear line of demarcation between the exploited peasantry and their exploiters.

If we keep all these shades of meaning in mind we will see how inappropriate it is to use the blanket term 'peasant society' to characterize whole civilizations like China and India. I believe that it is inappropriate to apply this term even to the rural sector of Indian society, although it might well cover the rural sector of other societies. As to individual rural communities, they have to be investigated in detail to see what part peasants play in their social and cultural life and with what other strata they co-exist.

For purposes of scientific discussion, clearly it is not enough to limit oneself to the popular meanings of basic concepts and categories. We shall now consider briefly two of the several definitions proposed by scholars of the categories which concern us. Fortunately these do not contradict the popular conceptions with which we started but help to give them rigour and precision.

Redfield, the pioneer among anthropologists in the field of peasant studies, urged caution in the formulation of definitions. He stressed their arbitrary nature as they were designed to comprehend clusters of real societies and cultures which differed somewhat among themselves. In other words, a definition of peasants formulated primarily on the basis of European experience would reflect European reality, and must therefore be used with caution in the study of Indian society. It is worth making this point because Indian anthropologists do not appear to have pondered sufficiently on the specific characteristics of Indian peasants and have assumed that they must be the same as those of peasants everywhere.

There are two major elements in Redfield's definition of peasants. The first specifies their mode of livelihood and the second their relationship to other strata. Peasants are, to begin with, 'small producers for their own consumption'.[3] But this conception, which Redfield attributes to Firth, is too broad, for it would include Malay fishermen at one end and Sioux hunters and gatherers at the other. Hence he would like to describe as peasants only those small producers 'who make a living and have a way of life through cultivation of the land'.[4] Further, following Eric Wolf, Redfield would like to confine the term peasants to those small agriculturists who produce

[3] Robert Redfield, *Peasant Society and Culture, An Anthropological Approach to Civilization*, University of Chicago Press, 1956. [4] Ibid., p. 18.

for their own consumption, describing as farmers those who produce for the market. He would also like to follow Wolf in limiting the term to those smallholding cultivators who control the land which they cultivate and are to that extent economically independent. When we turn to India with its elaborate tenurial arrangements we see at once the kind of problem this raises. Are tenants with occupancy rights peasants? What about sharecroppers, of whom there are several varieties even in a single state like West Bengal?

The second element in Redfield's definition places peasants in relational opposition to 'an elite of the manor, town or city'.[5] This corresponds to the opposition between peasantry and gentry to which we referred earlier. It is a significant indicator, with this important qualification that the elite or the gentry need not be 'of the manor, town or city', but may be a part of the village itself. In other words, I am arguing that the division between a lower stratum of peasants and an upper stratum of non-peasants might represent not a division between village and manor, or village and town, or village and city, but a cleavage within the village itself.

A more recent attempt to provide a definition is that of Teodor Shanin.[6] Shanin incorporates many of Redfield's ideas while adding a few others, and his definition is therefore more comprehensive. Besides the social and cultural characteristics of the peasantry, he also takes into account their political situation. But like Redfield, Shanin too tends to use the terms 'peasantry', 'peasant community' and 'peasant society' loosely and almost interchangeably.

Shanin describes what he calls peasant societies in terms of four basic facets which are as follows: '1. The peasant family farm as the basic unit of multidimensional social organization. . . . 2. Land husbandry as the main means of livelihood directly providing the major part of the consumption needs. . . . 3. Specific traditional culture related to the way of life of small communities. . . . 4. The underdog position—the domination of peasantry by outsiders'.[7] The second and third of these features do not call for any separate comment, hence I shall confine my observations to the first and the last.

The central significance of the peasant family as a unit of both consumption and production has of course been noted by many. In fact, nineteenth-century sociologists like Le Play and Tönnies would

[5] Ibid., p. 20.
[6] Teodor Shanin (ed.), *Peasants and Peasant Societies, Selected Readings*, Penguin, 1971, 'Introduction'.   [7] Ibid., pp. 14–15.

argue that the integral character of the family in work and leisure is what differentiates the peasant way of life from the industrial. However, when we define peasants in terms of the part played by the family on the farm, we must examine with some care the actual organization of work. When either the women or the men are customarily debarred from some or all forms of outdoor manual work, are we justified in describing them as peasants?

Shanin's last point, though introduced unobtrusively, represents a rather different perspective from that of Redfield. It derives from the Marxist or, more accurately, the Leninist tradition in sociology. The contrast between Redfield's and Lenin's perspectives on peasants reflects the difference between what Ossowski would describe as the 'functional' and the 'dichotomous' views of society.[8] The first view stresses the organic bonds between peasantry, gentry and other social strata while the second draws attention to the cleavage between an exploited class of peasants and their exploiters.

It is particularly interesting that in spite of this difference both Redfield and Shanin view the relationship between peasants and non-peasants as one between 'insiders' and 'outsiders'. For Redfield peasants in villages have their opposite numbers in 'the manor, town or city'; for Shanin peasants have an underdog position in which they are subjected to domination 'by outsiders'. Both seem to picture the village as the locus of a relatively homogeneous community of peasants.

The conceptual identity of village and peasant community is deeply rooted in both European scholarship and European ideology. Historians, jurists and economists writing about European countries have repeatedly characterized the village as a community of peasants. The same characterization—if anything in an even more extreme form—is found in the writings of European ideologues. The best example of this conceptual identification is to be found in the nineteenth century debate centring around the Russian *mir*, and its most forceful expression in the writings of the *narodniki*.

The writings of contemporary East European scholars from Mitrany to Georgescu-Roegen reveal the same point of view. Thus when Mitrany writes about the effects of land reforms in Rumania he treats the village and its peasants as interchangeable:[9] the village

[8] Stanislav Ossowski, *Class Structure in the Social Consciousness*, Routledge and Kegan Paul, 1963.
[9] David Mitrany, *The Land and the Peasant in Rumania, The War and Agrarian Reform (1917–21)*, O.U.P., 1930.

is where peasants live and those who live in the village are peasants. In a similar vein, in writing about 'Economic Theory and Agrarian Economics', Georgescu-Roegen equates village and peasant community.[10] He views the economic affairs of the village as being governed by rules that have a distinctive character by virtue of the intrinsic nature of peasant ways of life.

It is difficult to say how much of this identification of the village with its community of peasants in Europe is the result of an optical illusion. After all, what is highly differentiated internally often appears homogeneous at a distance. Those who wrote about village or peasant communities, whether of East or West Europe, were urban intellectuals—as Georgescu-Roegen has pointed out forcefully in regard to Marx.[11] It is not improbable that their notions about these communities should be slightly hazy and that they should invest the village with a little more homogeneity than it actually possessed. And even though the *narodniki* might have an intimate knowledge of peasant ways of life, they were clearly not writing about the Russian *mir* in the spirit of modern anthropologists.

Despite these reservations, one does have the general impression that the European village was in reality a relatively homogeneous and unstratified community. This was due in part to the manorial system which segregated the 'lord' in his manor from his 'peasants' in their village. Undoubtedly the European village varied greatly in its composition from one geographical region to another and from one historical period to the next. But social stratification was probably less a feature of the internal structure of the village than of its relation to the outside world.

It is difficult to say how far the European image of the peasant village influenced what British scholars and administrators perceived and wrote about the Indian village community before the days of intensive fieldwork. We have no reason to believe that Maine or Baden-Powell approached the Indian village without any preconceived notion of the kind of community a village would be. Nor can we say how intimate their knowledge was, judged by the standards of contemporary fieldwork, of the villages about which they wrote. They might well have approached village India with the belief, which Redfield held in more recent times, that peasants constitute 'the rural dimensions of old civilizations'.[12]

[10] N. Georgescu-Roegen, 'Economic Theory and Agrarian Economics', *Oxford Economic Papers*, Vol. 12, 1960, pp. 1–40.   [11] Ibid.
[12] Redfield, *Peasant Society and Culture*, op. cit., p. 20.

Whatever might be the true nature and composition of the European village, Redfield and Shanin have both provided useful definitions of the peasantry in which their simple and undifferentiated character is emphasized. Further, these definitions have the merit of being fairly close to the ordinary meanings of them. However, there are important sections of people in rural India—or in the Indian village—who do not fit this conception of the peasantry whichever way we look at it.

As we have seen, a peasant community, ideally conceived, is undifferentiated and unstratified. But what we learn from the many village studies now available is that the Indian village is often highly differentiated and generally stratified. This is far from saying that there are no peasants in the typical Indian village or even that there are no peasant villages in India; but it draws attention to the complex nature of rural society in India and to the varieties of villages in the country.

In order to make our argument clear we shall begin by examining an Indian village which is plainly not a community of peasants. This is an *agraharam* village which I have called Sripuram, in the Tanjore district of Tamil Nadu.[13] Although not representative in the statistical sense of the term, the *agraharam* village, of the kind exemplified by Sripuram, was by no means uncommon in this area even fifty years ago. Sounderaraja Iyengar mentions two principal kinds of villages, the *agraharavadai* dominated by Brahmins, and the *pandaravadai* dominated by the Non-Brahmins.[14] Of these the *pandaravadai* was clearly a closer approximation to the ideal type of a peasant village.

Sripuram is a large village of 349 households with a highly differentiated and stratified social structure. It is an ancient village, and its rich historical tradition is very much a part of the consciousness of at least the literate sections of its inhabitants. It has an ancient Shiva temple which bears inscriptions of the Chola kings of the eleventh century. It is, besides, a *padal sthalam*, or a place commemorated in song by the Shaiva *nayanmar* saints. In more recent times it has been associated with a disciple of the musician-saint Thyagaraja who contributed a distinctive mode of rendering classical Carnatic music named after the village.

Ninety-two of the 349 households in the village are of Brahmins,

[13] André Béteille, *Caste, Class, and Power: Changing Patterns of Stratification in a Tanjore Village*, University of California Press, 1965.

[14] S. Sounderaraja Iyengar, *Land Tenures in Madras Presidency*, Madras, 1933.

who all live in brick-and-tile houses in a separate street known as the *agraharam*. It is difficult to say how far the Brahmins of Sripuram correspond to a gentry in the European sense, but they cannot in any meaningful sense be grouped with the peasantry. They differ in almost every important respect—in food, habitation, dress and speech—from the peasants who are also a part of the village. And of course they are debarred by traditional sanctions from tilling the land which is the essential condition of the peasant's life.

The Brahmins of Sripuram and of other villages like it are known collectively as *mirasdars*. The Tanjore *mirasdar* is not only a landowner and rentier but also a man of leisure and cultivated taste. About ten years ago an article was published about the Tanjore *mirasdar*, presumably by one of the fraternity: 'In some instances, he had read widely, especially in Sanskrit. But mostly he preferred to stroll through life. Not for him the rude contact with labour. He preferred to watch and to contemplate. Yet he was not the social parasite that this may suggest. The fact was that he was rather the connoisseur of life, tasting it at many points.'[15] Here we get a vivid, if somewhat idyllic, picture of the Brahmin *mirasdar* of Tanjore in the early part of the century.

The Brahmins of Sripuram have pursued Sanskritic learning for centuries. Indeed their ancestors were settled in the village and granted land not in order to till but so as to be able to dedicate themselves to a life of learning, teaching and ritual. There are several families in the *agraharam* whose ancestors specialized in particular branches of Sanskritic learning. Not all the Brahmins in the village or even a majority of them are conversant with Sanskrit. But they are all equally conscious of their literary and classical heritage, placing a higher value on Sanskrit than on Tamil which is the language of their speech.

There are Brahmin villages like Sripuram throughout the country from Kashmir in the north to Tamil Nadu in the south, and from West Bengal in the east to Maharashtra in the west. Not all communities of Brahmins have kept up their heritage of Sanskritic learning, and they do not all have the same degree of 'culture', to use the term in its popular meaning. But everywhere there are ritual sanctions against their tilling the land which, as we have seen, is what makes a peasant what he is.

---

[15] Published in the Madras weekly, *Swarajya*, Vol. 5, 1961, No. 46, p. 13.

Brahmins are not the only category of people whose traditional style of life excluded the cultivation of land. Rajputs of proper caste and lineage were also debarred by ritual sanctions from using the plough. Further, the vast majority of Rajputs lived not in 'the manor, town or city' but in rural areas, as integral parts of village communities. Rajasthan is the state in which Rajputs are found in their most characteristic condition. Apart from the princes, *thikanedars* and *jagirdars*, there are communities of lesser Rajputs such as the *bhomias* of the Shekhawati area who have for centuries had their land cultivated by their tenants of lower caste.[16]

Some have suggested that the avoidance of ploughing and of manual work in general is based on the ritual attitudes towards purity and pollution and is therefore essentially a question of caste, but the matter is in fact more complex than that. Aristocratic and high status Muslims throughout rural India have shown an aversion for manual work which is as strong as that of the higher Hindu castes. In the villages of Burdwan district I encountered two categories of Muslims, the *ayamadar* or landlord, and *chashi* or peasant; the former kept their women in *purdah* and did not till the land. As is well known, these distinctions were even more marked in Uttar Pradesh and the former state of Hyderabad.

To come back to Sripuram, the village does not consist only of *mirasdar* Brahmins, and we must now take a look at some of the other sections of its population. The largest group of castes consists of a broad category described as Non-Brahmins and they include artisans as well as cultivators. There are three groups of 'cultivating castes' of which the principal ones are Vellalas, Kallas and Padayachis. In a broad sense it was the members of these groups who constituted the village peasantry, although they were tenants rather than owner-cultivators. Further, they were assisted, generally in the more rough and dirty work, by the Palla and Paraiya landless labourers.

In contrast to Sripuram is the village of Kila Ulur, situated in a different part of Tanjore district, described by Gilbert Étienne.[17] It seems to me that Kila Ulur may in a broad sense be described as a peasant village even though there are several different castes in it,

---

[16] I am grateful for the information on the *bhomias* to Anand Chakravarti. See his *Contradiction and Change*, Oxford University Press, 1975.

[17] Gilbert Etienne, *Studies in Indian Agriculture, The Art of the Possible*, University of California Press, 1968.

both Non-Brahmin and Harijan, and not all its households are of owner-cultivators. More than half of its economically active population consists of owner-cultivators and 'share-cropping is of small importance'[18] although there is a substantial population of landless labourers. Kila Ulur does not have Brahmin *mirasdars* or a separate stratum of rentiers of any other kind.

The Vellalas of Sripuram, the Kallas of Kila Ulur, the Okkaligas of Rampura and similar groups throughout the country are often described as 'cultivating' or 'peasant' castes. This blanket categorization has to be examined with care. For while the Brahmins of Tanjore and the Rajputs of Jaipur might be categorically described as non-cultivating or non-peasant castes since their traditional style of life excludes tillage, the larger castes of the middle level are too heterogeneous to be covered adequately by a blanket categorization.

When we come to castes such as the Vellalas of Tamil Nadu, the Sadgopes of West Bengal or the Marathas of Maharashtra, we have to take into account the internal differentiation and stratification that exists within each one of them. If our interest is in the agrarian social structure, then at the level of micro-analysis or of village studies we will have to treat in these cases not the caste or subcaste but the family or household as the unit of investigation and analysis. We will then probably find that some families of Vellalas (or of Sadgopes or of Marathas) are not peasants in the proper sense of the term, that others are clearly peasants and that yet others occupy a borderline position in terms of their actual role in production.

It was my experience during fieldwork in Burdwan district that some families of Sadgopes—whom I had till then viewed as a 'peasant' caste—did not participate in the actual work of tillage even when they lived in the village and owned holdings of only moderate size. They had their land cultivated either by share-croppers or by wage labourers. I later discovered that this withdrawal from the labour force was not a matter of personal idiosyncracy but was associated with socially-defined conceptions of status and family honour. Now when a number of related families have withdrawn from the actual work of tillage for at least two or three generations owing to discernible social causes, they have, in my view, ceased to be peasants.

If we direct our investigation to the family or household rather than the caste or subcaste, I am sure we will be able to discover

[18] Ibid., p. 207.

numerous such cases of 'lapsed peasants' among the so-called peasant castes throughout the country. This kind of investigation is also bound to reveal a large number of borderline cases of households whose status is from our point of view ambiguous. There will first of all be those families whose members have recently withdrawn from the labour force. They either give their land out to sharecroppers or have it tilled by wage labourers, engaging occasionally in actual farm work, and in other ways continuing to pursue a peasant style of life.

A more important factor behind this kind of ambiguity relates to the position of women in Indian society. As noted earlier, a peasant household in the true sense is one in which all its active members, both men and women, work on the farm. How are we to view families in which men work in the fields but women are by custom debarred from such work? Are these to be viewed as families of peasants or are they not? This question acquires particular importance in those forms of agriculture, such as wet paddy cultivation, which are based on an elaborate sexwise division of labour and in which the work cannot be completed without the participation of women. Sir Denzil Ibbetson's comment, 'The Jat calls himself *zamindar* or "husband-man" as often as Jat, and his women and children alike work with him in the fields'[19] may or may not hold for all Jat agriculturists, but it certainly does not hold for all families believed to be of peasant caste.

We have little precise information about the work done by women outside the home in the different strata of society in rural India. To the extent that we talk at all systematically about the organization of work in agriculture, we do so almost entirely from the man's point of view. This is unfortunate particularly because in India what women may or may not do is often a more sensitive indicator of family status than what is permitted or practised among men. It seems reasonable to maintain that a family of non-cultivating landowners moves down one step on the social ladder when its men go to work in the fields, but it comes down several steps when its women have to do the same. And if this is true of Hindus, it is even more true of Muslims.

[19] Cited in *Punjab Castes, Being a reprint of the chapter on 'The Races, Castes, and Tribes of the People' in the Report on the Census of the Punjab published in 1883 by the late Sir Denzil Ibbetson, K. C. S. I.*, Languages Department, Panjab, 1970, p. 103.

The whole process of status mobility, or what Srinivas describes as Sanskritization, can be examined in this light. When a family of proper peasants which has improved its economic position wishes to move up socially, it first withdraws its women from agriculture and then its men. One may even be able to trace out a regular sequence of steps. Women are first withdrawn from wage employment on the farms of others. They are then withdrawn from the family farm. Finally, the men either withdraw from work or change their role from cultivator to supervisor.

The role of women in Indian agriculture is particularly noteworthy because in this regard India seems to differ radically from the other major agrarian society, China. I am not referring here to China after the Communist revolution, which has evidently brought about great changes in the relations between the sexes, but about conditions in pre-Communist China. Admittedly our material on agricultural communities in traditional China is very limited, and our observations on this question must be made with caution and remain provisional. But whatever evidence we have seems to suggest that women played a much more active role on the family farm over a much wider range of the system of stratification in China than in India.

The few village studies that we have from China by Chinese anthropologists show that both men and women work actively on the farm. It is not as if these communities are totally unstratified, but such stratification as there is within the village does not take the form of a structural cleavage between families whose members work for themselves and others, and families for whom others work. In fact persons from even fairly prosperous families might work for wages for others who are less prosperous than they: these are proper communities of peasants.

It is not as if people never withdraw from farm work after becoming economically prosperous. But what Fei tells us is that in China it is the men who first withdraw in such cases, leaving the women to continue to work on the farm. 'The statement made previously that there is a tendency for landowners to avoid working on their farms might seem to be contradicted by the fact that women of all families, even those with large landholdings, are invariably active in agriculture. During the harvest period almost every woman in the village, except those occupied in cooking for the workers, is to be found toiling in the fields, while the little girls who are too young for farm work care for the babies.'[20]

Fei goes on to describe the case of a particular landowner who lived a life of leisure but had 'a pretty young daughter who could be found working in the fields, either on her father's or on some other farm, almost any day in the busy season.'[21] These observations appear so startling to a student of Indian society that he might doubt their authenticity had they not been supported by the authority of Fei Hsiao-Tung.

It is clear that Fei is not describing something accidental or peculiar to a particular village, for he has a theory to account for the unequal contribution of men and women to agricultural work. 'In the earlier discussion on farm labour I emphasized the fact that even in the very wealthy houses the women and girls work regularly in the fields. Although it may not seem fair that the weaker sex, with their bound feet, should toil in the mud while the men spend their days in idleness, an examination of property structure of the family makes it appear that there is a kind of balance and reciprocity in the household economy.'[22]

The argument, briefly speaking, is that since men (and not women) own the land, it is they who decide, naturally to their own advantage, who should be exempted from toil.

Fei's theory is not very satisfactory. Men own the land in India also, and presumably in India also it is they who decide which members of the family will be withdrawn from agricultural work in which order. But in this country it is the women and not the men who are the first to be withdrawn, and among wealthy, high status families there is never any question of women going out to work for wages on other people's land.

In reality the role of women in agriculture and the division of work in the peasant family as a whole are governed not merely by the structure of property rights, but also by a variety of conceptions such as those of status, honour and purity. These conceptions are culturally specific which means that they differ in their scope and significance from one society to another, and in the same society from one stratum to another. If we are to study peasant households

[20] Fei Hsiao-Tung and Chang Chih-I, *Earthbound China, A Study of Rural Economy in Yunnan*, Routledge and Kegan Paul, 1949, p. 65.
[21] Ibid., p. 66.   [22] Ibid., p. 111.

or peasant communities in a more meaningful way, we will have to devote more serious attention to these beliefs, values and sentiments, particularly when we are comparing one society with another.

The purity of women in Hindu society is a subject in itself, and it has been discussed elaborately and at length in the context of marriage rules and practices.[23] It has not been discussed so far by sociologists in a systematic way in the context of extra-domestic work, particularly the type of work which involves the joint participation of men and women. It is generally known that the concepts of purity and pollution debar members of certain castes from tilling the land while allowing others to do it. We are likely to get a more differentiated picture of the domestic economy if we remember that the concepts of purity and pollution apply differently to men and to women.

If the concept of ritual purity is specific to Hinduism, that of social honour is more general, applying to both Hindus and Muslims, though perhaps in somewhat different ways. The institution of *purdah* has for centuries been the hallmark of status among Muslims in India, and among poorer Muslims of aristocratic pretensions it been and continues to be a severe strain on the economic resources of the family. Among the Hindus, similar considerations govern the Rajput style of life, and, as is well known, families with claims to Rajput status are a common feature of the entire Hindi-speaking region.

We have come a long way from the facile assumption that all those who live in villages, men and women, may be described as peasants. The population of the Indian village is often highly stratified and some of these strata are clearly different from peasants in any sense of the term. While we do get a broad notion of this order of stratification from a consideration of caste, this is not enough. In order to get a more accurate picture, particularly of groups at the middle of the hierarchy, we have to take the family as the unit and to examine in particular the division of work between men and women within and outside the domestic sphere.

There are different types of villages in India. Some clearly are peasant villages, whereas in others non-peasants co-exist with peasants and may even predominate over them, if not in numbers at

[23] Nur Yalman, 'On the Purity of Women in the Castes of Ceylon and Malabar', *Journal of the Royal Anthropological Institute*, Vol. 93, Part 1, 1963, pp. 25–8.

least in social, economic and political influence. It is possible that villages of different types predominate in different regions, although each major region will have several types of villages.

The point which I would like to emphasize in conclusion is the co-existence of 'peasantry' and 'gentry' as a common feature of many Indian villages and a characteristic feature of some. This is at variance with the European conception of the village and perhaps also the European reality. But in order to be able to say anything with confidence on this question we need a much fuller investigation of the facts. It is my belief that the vague and imprecise concept of 'peasant society', which has gained currency among sociologists and social anthropologists, stands as an obstacle in the way of this kind of investigation.

The most interesting comparison is not between India and Europe, but between India and China. We have already seen that there are certain differences between these two major Asian countries in their traditional productive organizations. The attitudes towards the place of women on the farm are clearly different in the two countries, if we can go by Fei's testimony and our own observations. Further, all the villages studied by Chinese anthropologists are or closely approximate to peasant communities whereas this is by no means the case in India, although this difference may be partly due to the criteria adopted in the selection of the two sets of villages.

The apparent predominance of peasant villages in China may be related to a significant observation made by Fei. In a discussion of peasantry and gentry in China, Fei maintains that there is not only a social but an ecological separation between the two. He remarks, 'The peasantry and gentry can further be contrasted by showing their ecological positions.'[24] There is little scope for peasants to improve their economic position within the village. 'Therefore, it is essential for the rich to keep away from the village. The place where they can maintain their power and wealth is the town.'[25] While towns have certainly been important centres of civilization in India, there has always been ample scope within the village itself for the rich to maintain their power and wealth.

---

[24] Fei Hsiao-Tung, 'Peasantry and Gentry in China, An Interpretation of Chinese Social Structure and its Changes' in Reinhard Bendix and Seymour Martin Lipset (eds.), *Class, Status and Power, A Reader in Social Stratification*, Routledge and Kegan Paul, 1954, p. 637.
[25] Ibid.

4
Tribe and Peasantry

A NUMBER OF different streams of scholarship have contributed to the study of peasants. Historians, economists and social anthropologists have enriched our knowledge of peasant social structure and culture in various ways. One may observe certain differences in the characterization of the peasantry offered by scholars pursuing these different disciplines. This is partly, and at least on the surface, due to differences in the empirical material on which they have worked. But it is no less due to differences in the conceptual schemes and theoretical questions which they have brought to the study of the peasantry from their respective disciplines.

In this chapter the contribution made to peasant studies primarily by the anthropological stream will be examined. The most notable feature of this contribution lies in the richness of the empirical material it brought into the analysis of the peasantry. This empirical material was not only very rich, but was of an altogether new kind. Here were scholars who were for the first time studying peasants by living among them, and examining systematically and in detail the various facets of peasant life as it was actually lived.

However, we must not forget that anthropologists had first specialized in the study of tribes before they undertook the study of peasants. Their stock of theories, concepts and methods had acquired shape in the course of their studies of primitive, pre-literate or tribal communities, and it was only natural that these should influence to some extent not only their investigation of peasant communities, but also their characterization of them. Hence in order to understand how anthropologists came to view peasants we must know a little about how they had earlier come to view tribes.

The first anthropological studies of village communities in complex societies were viewed outside the profession with some misgiving if not suspicion. I was told by a distinguished Japanese scholar that the weakness of Embree's study of Suye Mura[1] was that it made the Japanese village appear like a primitive tribal community. The burden of this kind of criticism is that the internal structure of a Japanese village (or an Indian village) has an order of complexity which is quite different from what one encounters in a tribal community.

It is not that anthropologists were unaccustomed to dealing with complex structural problems, but their work in tribal societies had trained them to seek out only some and not all types of complexity. To be specific, anthropologists were highly skilled at identifying and analysing kinship and lineage structures, but on the whole somewhat inept at handling class and social stratification. For this reason they often ignored or paid insufficient attention to the structure of inequalities, at least in their earlier village studies. As a consequence, villages of very different kinds all came to be regarded as communities of peasants. The resulting ambiguity can be easily seen in the anthropological literature on the peasantry. We are told, for instance, that 'the peasant village is heterogeneous in terms of internal division into caste and class'.[2] It is unlikely that an economist or a historian who is used to viewing peasants as a class or a stratum would write in this way. For if the peasants are treated as a particular class, then the term 'peasant' cannot be applied to a community which is internally divided into diverse classes.

But this represents only one side of the coin. For if anthropologists have implicitly viewed peasant communities in terms of tribal categories, they have also been unusually keen to distinguish explicitly between 'tribe' and 'peasant'. One can go even further and say that if there is something distinctive in the anthropologist's characterization of the peasantry, it derives from the way in which he contrasts the two sociological types. The economist or historian on the other hand has not viewed 'tribe' and 'peasant' as mutually exclusive categories.

If one were to approach the study of the peasantry as an economic historian, one might characterize peasants by contrasting them not with tribesmen but with the other classes or strata in a complex society. It is not that social anthropologists have completely ignored

---

[1] John F. Embree, *A Japanese Village: Suye Mura*, Routledge and Kegan Paul, 1946.
[2] Surajit Sinha, 'Tribe-Caste and Tribe-Peasant Continua in Central India', *Man in India*, Vol. 45, No. 1, 1965, p. 62.

the relationship between peasants and other social strata. Redfield, for instance, saw the importance of the distinction between peasantry and gentry within the framework of a complex society. But in defining the characteristics of what he called peasant society he placed much greater emphasis on its contrast with tribal society.[3]

There is clearly a difference between contrasting peasants with tribesmen and contrasting peasantry with gentry. In the first case we are, as it were, contrasting two different types of society whereas in the second we are contrasting two strata within the same society. It can be shown that many anthropologists talk about tribe and peasant as though they constituted different societies. This creates problems when we are dealing with societies of the Indian kind where tribes, peasantry and gentry constitute elements within one and the same society.

It has to be admitted that there is something basically unsatisfactory about the scheme adopted by Redfield and his followers which divides Indian society into three sectors, tribal, peasant and urban.[4] The three terms in the scheme are logically disparate. Clearly, one can think of an alternative scheme in which the three terms would be tribesmen, peasantry and gentry. One might then find that the difference between tribesmen and peasants in India is in general much smaller than the difference between either of them and the gentry.

It is no doubt possible to use the labels 'tribal' and 'peasant' for two types of social organization and to characterize one by contrasting it with the other. But in spite of all the effort invested by anthropologists in the study of primitive societies, there really is no satisfactory way of defining a tribal society. What this amounts to in the Indian context is that anthropologists have tried to characterize a somewhat nebulous sociological type by contrasting it with another which is almost equally nebulous. Earlier anthropologists had not paid sufficient attention to the definition of tribal society, but tacitly assumed that what they were studying in Australia, Melanesia and Africa were various forms of tribal society. The tribe was somewhat vaguely assumed to be a more or less homogeneous society having a common government, a common dialect and a common culture. Since Evans-Pritchard's time[5] anthropologists have tried in a much

[3] Robert Redfield, *Peasant Society and Culture*, University of Chicago Press, 1956.
[4] This scheme was adopted at a seminar organized in Chicago by Robert Redfield, Milton Singer and Surajit Sinha under the auspices of the Ford Foundation in 1956.
[5] E. E. Evans-Pritchard, *The Nuer*, Clarendon Press, 1940.

more systematic way to provide a structural definition of the tribe, particularly in the context of segmentary societies.

However, as I. M. Lewis indicates, it is one thing to show how boundaries should be drawn between different tribes, and another to specify the characteristics of tribal societies as such. Lewis himself proposes the criterion of 'scale', introduced into anthropology by Godfrey and Monica Wilson,[6] to define the nature of societies of this kind. 'Ideally, tribal societies are small in scale, are restricted in the spatial and temporal range of their social, legal and political relations, and possess a morality, religion and world view of corresponding dimensions.'[7] Two comments may be made on this. Firstly, some of the major Indian tribes such as the Santals, Gonds and Bhils are quite large, numbering over a million persons each and scattered over extensive territories. Secondly, if we are considering not the tribe as a whole but 'tribal' communities, it can be shown that there are 'peasant' communities in many parts of the world which are also 'small in scale'.

A rather more interesting characterization of tribal society is the one provided by Sahlins[8] which can be traced back to the writings of scholars such as Durkheim and Mauss.[9] Sahlins has argued that the term 'tribal society' be restricted to what are called segmentary systems. Segmentary systems are not only small in scale but represent a definite structural type which is quite different from the more complex social systems in which peasantry and gentry coexist. If we define 'tribe' in this sense we will find that the Santals, Oraons and Mundas correspond less to tribes than to what are broadly described as peasants.

There is thus no one way of defining tribal society. Definitions may be either very broad and loose or very narrow and restricted. The former would apply not only to tribes but in many ways also to the peasantry. The latter would exclude many societies which have been conventionally regarded as tribal. It will no doubt be argued that the definition of a tribal society as a segmentary system will not be of much practical use in a country like India where segmentary societies cannot be easily identified. Bailey is perhaps the only

[6] Godfrey and Monica Wilson, *The Analysis of Social Change*, Cambridge University Press, 1945.
[7] I. M. Lewis, 'Tribal Society' in David L. Sils (ed.), *International Encyclopedia of the Social Sciences*, The Macmillan Company and The Free Press, 1968, Vol. 16, p. 147.
[8] Marshall D. Sahlins, *Tribesmen*, Prentice-Hall, 1968.
[9] See Marcel Mauss, *Oeuvres*, Vol. III, Les Editions de Minuit, 1969, pp. 580 ff.

anthropologist working in the Indian field who has tried to characterize tribes in terms of segmentary principles, but the contrast in which he is interested is not between 'tribe' and 'peasant' but between 'tribe' and 'caste'.[10]

Unlike Bailey, the majority of Indian anthropologists have not given much serious thought to the problem of creating a definition of tribal society which will be appropriate to the Indian context. Rather they appear to have wavered continually between textbook definitions of 'tribe' and prevailing classifications of Indian society into 'tribal' and 'non-tribal'. Even if we are not able to settle once and for all what we must mean by 'tribal society' or how the term ought to be used in India, it should be worthwhile to examine the context of its use in Indian society.

The convention to categorize certain groups in Indian society as tribal was established during the nineteenth century largely by British administrators. From the 1930's onwards lists began to be prepared of Indian tribes with a view to giving them administrative and political concessions. The list of Scheduled Tribes attached to the Constitution of India had its origins in these. It cannot be too strongly emphasized that the list reflects the demands more of administrative and political circumstance than of academic or logical rigour. As a consequence the same groups might be treated as a tribe in one state but not in another. It is not surprising that Government should have a list of this kind in the interest of practical policy. What is surprising is that since independence anthropologists have more or less accepted the list without critically examining its rationale.

A notable feature of British administration in India was the task assigned to the decennial census operations. This included not only the counting of heads but the classification of the population into various categories. The successive census operations resulted in the creation of an enormously complex system of categories for dividing the population into tribes, castes, sects and occupations. Several of the earlier officials in charge of census operations were men with a passion for ethnology, and this no doubt contributed to the complexity of the categorical apparatus they created.[11]

Since our existing list of tribes derives largely from the work of

---

[10] F. G. Bailey, ' "Tribe" and "Caste" in India', *Contributions to Indian Sociology*, No. V, 1961, pp. 7-19.

[11] R. Saumerez Smith, *Caste, Religion and Locality in the Punjab Census*, M. Litt. dissertation submitted to the University of Delhi, 1971.

these census officials, it would be only fair to say that they were not much concerned with the distinction between 'tribe' and 'peasant'. Initially they used the term 'tribe' in a rather loose sense, using it frequently to describe groups such as the Jats and Ahirs. But by the time of the 1931 census, of which J. H. Hutton was in over-all charge, the distinction between 'tribe' and 'caste' had become an issue of some importance. Tribes came to be viewed more and more in religious and not just ecological terms. If a group could be shown to be clearly 'Hindu' in its religious beliefs and practices, it was a caste; if it was 'Animist' it had to be treated as a tribe.

It is erroneous to argue that 'Animists' cannot be peasants. For by doing so the word 'peasant' would be given a very peculiar meaning. Hence for the time being we should set aside altogether the scheme which divides Indian society into tribal, peasant and urban, and examine to what extent and in what sense our tribal people can also be regarded as peasants.

India has probably the largest tribal population of any country in the world, if we go by the official classification. Apart from the large size of this population—over thirty million in 1971—its most striking feature is its enormous diversity. The tribal people are to be found in various parts of the country, although there are large concentrations of them in particular regions. One of the notable features of this distribution, which represents an ancient pattern, is that at least outwardly the tribal people of one particular region often resemble more closely the non-tribal people of that region than the tribal people of another region.

There is no single way of making a satisfactory classification of the 427 tribes found in India. I propose to follow here the classification adopted by N. K. Bose. 'There are many ways in which tribes can be classified. One, as we have already said, is by language; another is by religion; a third is by the degree of isolation to which they are subject, which has led some to retain a larger proportion of their original culture than others. But, we believe, the plainest way will be to arrange them into categories based on the manner in which they primarily make their living.'[12] For a discussion which seeks to inquire whether tribes can also be regarded as peasants, this is obviously the most satisfactory procedure. Bose divides the tribal people into three principal categories, (i) hunters, fishers and

[12] N. K. Bose, *Tribal Life in India*, New Delhi, 1971, pp. -5.

gatherers; (ii) shifting cultivators; and (iii) settled agriculturists using the plough and plough cattle. He lists two other categories, viz. nomadic cattle keepers, artisans and labourers; and workers in plantations and industries. Among these it is the settled agriculturists using the plough and plough cattle who account for the overwhelming majority of the tribal people; the workers in plantations and industries are also recruited mainly from their ranks.

The larger tribes which number over a million persons each—the Santals, Gonds, Bhils, Oraons and Mundas—are all settled agriculturists and have been so for generations. Their members are today 'classified under the categories of cultivators, agricultural labourers and workers in certain other primary types of occupation'.[13] Bose has revealed the presence of a simple but definite division of labour in their villages. Thus one can find in these tribal villages, in addition to cultivators, households specializing in such crafts as basket-making, oil-pressing and blacksmithery—all necessary elements in an economy of land and grain.

My first exposure as a fieldworker to the tribal people of India was in Ranchi district where I made observations in an Oraon village in 1956–7. Later I was able to observe Santal villages in Hazaribagh district in the course of a survey made under the auspices of the Indian Statistical Institute. Although these exposures were brief and I spent just a month studying material culture, social organization and religion in an Oraon village in Ranchi district, I came away with the strong impression that the inhabitants of these villages corresponded very closely to the ordinary meaning of peasants. I clearly remember my initial disappointment in discovering that, although we had come to investigate proper tribals, the people who confronted us were outwardly no different from the poorer villagers one might find anywhere in rural Bihar or West Bengal. The Oraon inhabitants of the village in Ranchi district which I had investigated fit very well into Shanin's conception of the peasantry discussed in the previous chapter.[14] It seems to me that they fit this conception much better than the people of the village in Tanjore district I investigated five years later. It will be useful to take up the main points in Shanin's conception and see in a general way whether they apply to the inhabitants of the Oraon, Munda, Ho and Santal villages of Chota Nagpur.

[13] Ibid., p. 23.
[14] Teodor Shanin (ed.), *Peasants and Peasant Societies*, Penguin, 1971, Introduction.

The first characteristic of the peasantry is the central importance of the family farm. Although the clan and the lineage have been, and continue to be, important structural units among the agricultural tribes of Chota Nagpur, it is really the family which is the principal unit of both production and consumption. Individual families act as units of production on land which they themselves control (as 'cultivators') or on land owned and controlled by others (as sharecroppers or agricultural labourers). In either case both men and women participate jointly in agricultural work, contrary to the practice of high status families among Hindus and Muslims, including families belonging to the so-called cultivating castes.

Secondly, not only do these families engage in settled agriculture but land husbandry constitutes for them the main means of livelihood and provides for the major part of their consumption needs. Almost all these tribes have myths which speak of an earlier phase when they lived by hunting and gathering and which make a symbolic assertion of the place of these activities in their culture. But it is difficult to translate these myths into historical terms, and clearly these tribes have lived by settled agriculture for at least five generations and probably longer. Further, their agriculture has been primarily a subsistence agriculture, although it may be rash to assert that they have had no links with markets.

The third point in Shanin's characterization of the peasantry is about their 'specific traditional culture related to the way of life of small communities'.[15] What Shanin has in mind are features such as conformity to age-old habits and practices and the subordination of the individual to the community. As he rightly points out, these follow more or less from life in fairly small and stable local communities. Once again, if we were to look for these features in rural India, the Santal, Oraon or Munda village would be a good place in which to begin.

Finally, we have what Shanin calls the 'underdog position' of the peasantry, or their domination by outsiders. Peasants occupy, as it were by definition, a subordinate position in all stratified societies, but the extent of their exploitation varies greatly from one society to another, and within the same society from one region to another. I have argued that peasants are not necessarily exploited by 'outsiders'; their exploiters in the highly-stratified Indian village are often other

---

[15] Ibid., p. 15.

strata of the village itself. But if there is any single category of Indian peasants who have been exploited from 'outside' for over a century, it is the Oraon, Munda and Santal villagers of Chota Nagpur, and tribal agriculturists in India as a whole.

One important reason why the exploiters of these tillers of the land—moneylenders, revenue farmers, landlords—are mainly outsiders is that the Santal, Oraon, Ho or Munda village is itself relatively homogeneous and unstratified. It is, above all, in this sense that these villages are to be viewed as true communities of peasants. Economic inequalities no doubt exist in these villages, but they are of a totally different order from the inequalities present in villages where Brahmin or Rajput or Muslim landlords reside.

Our general impression of the peasant economy of the larger tribes of Chota Nagpur has of course to be tested by a detailed and systematic examination of the facts. This is particularly necessary if we are to avoid making general statements about tribes which will be as vast and empty as the ones about peasants we commented upon in the previous chapter. India has a large number of tribes which, as we saw earlier, differ very much from each other, and while some correspond to peasants, others do not. What is more important is that a single 'tribe' such as the Bhil or the Gond sometimes turns out to be an aggregate of many sections, some clearly being peasants and others, equally clearly, being not.

Unfortunately, detailed studies of tribal communities in their traditional context are no longer made as widely as in the past. The trend in the last two decades has been to replace tribal monographs with 'village studies'. What is remarkable about this shift in interest among Indian anthropologists is that 'village studies' are viewed as different from or alternative to 'tribal studies', whereas in fact one could very well make studies of 'tribal' villages just as studies of non-tribal villages are made. There is little doubt that this way of contrasting 'tribal studies' with 'village studies' is a direct consequence of the false opposition between 'tribe' and 'peasant' which was imposed on Indian anthropology in the middle fifties.

It is difficult to account satisfactorily for the decline of interest among anthropologists in the study of tribal communities. During the last two decades barely half-a-dozen good monographs have appeared on Indian tribes, and even these are not all studies of tribes in their 'natural' setting. It is quite understandable that so much attention should be devoted to the study of peasants by Indian anthropologists. But there is no reason why this should be done at the expense of tribal studies, particularly when so many of India's tribal communities are in fact communities of peasants.

In the absence of good recent studies on the social and economic life of the cultivating tribes, we have to go back to the monographs published by earlier scholars from S. C. Roy to C. von Fürer-Haimendorf. Unfortunately those monographs were written before the strategy of intensive village studies came to be commonly adopted by anthropologists. Most of them provide generalized accounts of the materials traits, social institutions and religious practices of the various tribes. Few of them give us the kind of detailed information, at the level of the local community, that we have for the non-tribal people in our rural areas. One of the interesting aspects of these earlier monographs is that they appear not to view 'tribe' and 'peasant' as mutually exclusive categories. S. C. Roy speaks freely of the Oraon and Munda villagers as peasants, and Fürer-Haimendorf describes the 'peasant' culture of the Raj Gonds of Adilabad. In more recent times Bailey has characterized the Konds of Orissa as peasants.

S. C. Roy's account of the Oraons, published nearly sixty years ago, provides valuable data on agriculture from the viewpoint of both material culture and social organization. Although we are not presented with a detailed description of any particular village, there is much information on the nature of village organization, including the organization of economic life. The village economy of the Oraons is essentially an economy of land and grain, although ancillary occupations are also practised by both Oraon and non-Oraon inhabitants of the village. The principal crop grown by the Oraons is paddy, although two varieties of millets, *gondli* and *marua*, are also grown and form an important ingredient in the diet of the poorer Oraons. Paddy cultivation is technologically a very complex process. Roy gives us detailed descriptions of the various operations involved—manuring, ploughing, regulation of water, sowing, transplanting, weeding, harvesting[16]—which are similar even on points of detail to the operations performed by non-tribal peasants in the plains of Bihar and West Bengal. Roy also gives us an account of the division of labour between men and women in

---

[16] Sarat Chandra Roy, *The Oraons of Chota Nagpur*, Ranchi, 1915, pp. 123–8.

Oraon agriculture. Women do the transplanting and weeding, men do the hoeing, ploughing, levelling and sowing while harvesting is done by both men and women;[17] here again there is a detailed similarity between Oraon agriculture and the agriculture of non-tribal peasants.

Roy's description of the composition of an Oraon village deserves to be quoted at length. 'A typical Oraon village thus consists of the Bhuinhars, subsequent Oraon settlers (called Jeth-raiyats or ordinary raiyats, according as they are earlier or later settlers) and a Gorait family, one or two Ahir families, a Lohra family, and sometimes also a family of Kumhars. In many villages, a few families of Ghasis, Jolahas or in some cases Chik Baraiks (weavers), and Mahalis (basket-makers) and a few other castes and tribes are also met with.'[18] There are two points in this description which should be particularly noted: (i) the differentiation of Oraons according to their tenurial status and (ii) the presence of both Hindu and Muslim groups of artisans.

The core of the Oraon village, according to Roy, consists of the Bhuinhars whom he characterizes as 'peasant proprietors'.[19] He believes that there was a stage in the past when these peasant proprietors were fully independent, without 'landlords over their heads', and without 'rents or taxes to pay'.[20] We do not have good historical material to be able to say when, if at all, such a condition prevailed. But by the time Roy started his investigation of the Oraons at the beginning of the twentieth century there were already among them various categories of *raiyats*, a term used throughout India to characterize cultivators or peasants. That the Oraon village at the turn of the century was not a simple tribal community is confirmed by the regular presence in it of members of various endogamous groups. The identity of these is not always easy to establish, and perhaps it is not very pertinent to ask whether groups such as the Mahalis, Ghasis and Lohras are Hinduized tribals or tribalized Hindus. From our point of view, their presence contributed just that much of heterogeneity and stratification which seems to be a characteristic feature of peasant communities throughout the world.

The Mundas of Chota Nagpur are generally believed to be older

[17] Ibid., p. 131.
[18] Ibid., pp. 110–11.
[19] Ibid., p. 109.
[20] Ibid.

inhabitants of the area than the Oraons and to be agriculturally somewhat more backward. Nevertheless, they also have an economic system and a village organization which are basically similar to those of the Oraons. They are settled cultivators, having a characteristically peasant division of labour within the family, and they live in villages along with artisans who supply their basic non-agricultural requirements.

Some interest has centred around what is known as the *khuntkatti* tenure among the Mundas, and a brief description of the *khuntkatti* village as it was seen at the beginning of the twentieth century would be useful. In a special contribution to the *Encyclopaedia Mundarica*, Hoffman and Lister write: 'The pure Mundari *khuntkatti* village usually contains three elements, namely (a) the *khuntkattidars*, (b) the *parjas* or raiyats, and (c) the subsidiary castes. The *khuntkattidars* are the descendants in the male line of the original founders of the village... The *parjas* are almost invariably Mundaris, and very often are relatives on the female side of the *khuntkattidars*.... The subsidiary castes (Penrains, Mahilis or Khangars, Bhogtas, and Barais) perform the non-agricultural functions necessary to the village life and rarely cultivate land.'[21] The authors of the article hasten to add that pure *khuntkatti* villages are becoming scarce and proceed to give a description of what they call 'broken *khuntkatti* villages'. The breakdown of *khuntkatti* villages has been associated with two factors: (i) the emergence of individual ownership of land as opposed to control by the local lineage and (ii) the encroachment of moneylenders and landlords into the Munda country. We do not know how effective the control of the lineage was over the holdings operated by particular families, and exactly when this control began to loosen. Nor is it true that landlords and moneylenders were completely unknown in the area before the advent of British rule.

Fürer-Haimendorf's study of the Raj Gonds of Adilabad relates to a more recent period. Although this is a different area from Chota Nagpur, we note here also the same three elements in the population: (i) 'the so-called "aboriginals" ', divided into various endogamous groups and living mainly by agriculture, (ii) 'the associated castes of bards, musicians and craftsmen', and (iii) castes of Telugu and Marathi extraction, and Muslims who have come mainly

---

[21] J. Hoffmann and E. Lister, 'Special Memorandum on the Land System of the Munda Country' in J. Hoffmann (in collaboration with A. van Emelen), *Encyclopaedia Mundarica*, Vol. VIII, Patna, 1950, p. 2389.

from outside.[22] While there is some amount of ecological separation between the three categories of people, villages in which the Raj Gonds live are also frequently inhabited by members of the second category. Fürer-Haimendorf takes care to point out that in Adilabad district 'the Raj Gonds do not form a ruling class or even a class of privileged economic status, but an entire tribal group comprising all strata of society from the feudal chiefs down to the poorest labourer'.[23] The Raj Gonds are jealous of their cultural identity which they seek to protect in various ways. But this form of syncretic unity—we may call it tribal identity if we wish—does not negate the diacritical unity which the Raj Gond cultivators share with cultivators belonging to other groups in the area.

We know of various types of economic systems among the Raj Gonds in terms of both technology and social organization. Shifting cultivation was widely practised in the area in earlier times and was common even in the forties. But in addition to millets, the Raj Gonds were also growing wheat and cotton. These tribal people are not only peasants but they are peasants who are now becoming increasingly articulated with a market economy.

One way of meeting my argument would be to say that while it is true that a substantial number of tribal people are peasants today, this is because we no longer have tribes in their pure state but only tribes in transition. The notion of the Indian tribes being in a state of transition was raised for systematic inquiry by Professor D. N. Majumdar nearly forty years ago.[24] Since then it has become a kind of stock-in-trade for most anthropologists writing about the tribal situation in India. There can be no question but that major changes have been taking place among India's tribal people in the course of the last hundred years. Their isolation has broken down or been reduced. In many areas shifting cultivators have become settled agriculturists using the plough and plough cattle. With changes in technology there have come about corresponding changes in their organization of production. Patterns of landholding have changed. The lineage is less important as a corporate group than it was in the

[22] C. von Fürer-Haimendorf (in collaboration with E. von Fürer-Haimendorf), *The Raj Gonds of Adilabad, A Peasant Culture of the Deccan*, Book I, MacMillan and Co., 1948, p. 31.

[23] Ibid., p. 5.

[24] D. N. Majumdar, *A Tribe in Transition, A Study in Culture Pattern*, Longmans, 1937.

past, and the market economy is altering not only the relationship of the tribal village with the outside world but also the economic and social structure of the village itself.

Unfortunately, the notion of 'transition' is in sociology a rather elusive one, and it is used as often to evade an argument as to confirm it. The more closely we look into the social institutions of the tribes like the Oraons, Mundas and Santhals, the more we are likely to find that they have been in transition for a period which is to be measured not in decades but in centuries. Reliable historical material on these tribes does not go very far back in time, and in any case the conditions under which their history comes to be recorded are precisely those which are associated with a transition in their life.

N. K. Bose writes about the Mundas: 'It is not unlikely that in the past the Kol or Munda tribe practised some form of slash-and-burn agriculture. Even now one might find among them vague memories of the forest being gradually cleared by burning or *jara*.'[25] However, Bose does not fail to point out that 'our earliest records of the Mundas show them as settled in permanent villages and practising plough cultivation in the uplands'.[26] These records go back to the end of the eighteenth century. Bose shows how the traditional *khuntkatti* village had begun to disintegrate during the period of Muslim rule. If the Mundas had ever been, in S. C. Roy's phrase, 'peasant proprietors' at some stage, their independence had begun to be whittled down with the emergence of a state structure in the seventeenth century itself. 'In order to enhance the splendour of the Chota Nagpur court, the king began to adorn it with Kshatriya and Brahmin attendants with titles such as *rautiya, bhaiya, brittiya, pandeya, jamadar, wohdar*, etc., and a new economic arrangement was started, based on the *jagir* system which was introduced for the maintenance of these immigrant courtiers. The oldest document recovered from the royal treasury is dated 1676.'[27]

In other words, what some would call the 'underdog position' of the Munda peasantry, or their 'exploitation by outsiders' is at least three hundred years old.

This chapter began by arguing that in the Indian context it does not seem justifiable to define 'tribe' in opposition to 'peasant' since

[25] Nirmal Kumar Bose, *Hindu Samajer Garhan*, Vishwabharati Granthalaya, 1356 (Bengali calendar), p. 19.
[26] Ibid., p. 18.   [27] Ibid., p. 24.

a substantial number of tribal people are in fact peasants and have been so for a long time. Further, the accepted meaning of the phrase does not require that peasants should adhere to any particular religion; in other words, peasants may be Muslim, Christian, Hindu or Animist. This brings us to our final question, which is whether the tribal people mentioned earlier can also be regarded as Hindus. Putting it a little differently, even if it is true that the Santals, Mundas and Oraons are peasants, one might ask if there are not substantial differences between them and the other Indian peasants who are clearly Hindus.

I would like to make it clear that the true object of sociology is not to impose a kind of unity on social phenomena, but to seek, at one and the same time, both similarities and differences among them. My purpose in drawing attention to the 'tribal' peasantry is not to establish an identity between them and the non-tribal peasantry, but to argue that the similarities between, say, Bhumij and Kurmi peasants in the economic and political spheres is probably much greater than the similarities between either and, say, Brahmin or Rajput landlords.

Hence, even if we dismiss the contrast between tribe and peasant as being largely misleading in the Indian context, we are still left with the contrast between tribe and caste. Anthropologists have differed sharply on this question. Ghurye has been of the opinion that the tribal people are 'backward Hindus', differing only in degree from the other segments of Hindu society.[28] Elwin, on the other hand, has argued forcefully and eloquently for the recognition of the separate social and cultural identity of the tribal people.[29] The Government of India, it must be noted, gives tacit recognition to this identity by keeping alive under Constitutional sanction its list of Scheduled Tribes.

There are certain commonly-observed differences between tribes and castes which may be considered briefly. There is first the relative isolation of tribes as compared with castes. This has two facets. It means, first, that the tribes are geographically isolated, being concentrated in areas which are or have been more or less inaccessible. It also means—and this is for the sociologist more important—that a tribe is a world within itself having few external

[28] G. S. Ghurye, *The Aborigines—'so-called'—and their Future*, Gokhale Institute of Politics and Economics, 1943.
[29] V. Elwin, *The Aboriginals*, O.U.P., 1943.

social ties, whereas a caste is by its nature a part of a larger whole being linked by multifarious ties with other castes.

The second criterion is language or dialect. The tribes speak a variety of dialects which can be shown to differ on a number of important counts from the major Indian languages. This is the really crucial diacritical feature which separates 'tribal' from 'non-tribal' peasants when they come to live together in the same region, district or village. But here also there is some ambiguity. For even if we take a restricted area like Chota Nagpur we will find that there are tribes like the Oraons and Mundas which speak quite different dialects, and that there are yet others like the Bhumij who have lost their tribal dialect and now use the dominant language of the area.

In the end there is religion. Even if we regard the contrast between 'Animism' and 'Hinduism' as too crude, we might concede that there are numerous elements of religious belief and practice common to Oraons, Santals, Mundas and Hos which do not find a place in what is commonly accepted as Hinduism. But religion, unlike language, is a loose criterion, for what we encounter is a continuum without sharp breaks, and where we draw the line between 'tribal' and 'non-tribal' must remain arbitrary. N. K. Bose, who combined the perspectives of ethnography and Indology in his study of tribe and caste, was inclined to stress the continuity between the two. What he says about shifting cultivators like Juangs and Savaras deserves our attention for it applies *a fortiori* to settled agriculturists like Mundas, Oraons and Santals. 'Now, in this context the question arises as to whether groups such as the Juangs and Savaras should or should not be regarded as a part of Hindu society, or, in other words, of the social organization based on caste. Popular opinion in the state of Pal Lahara would say that even though the Juangs speak a non-Aryan language and eat the flesh of cows, pigs, snakes and other unclean animals, they ought to be counted among the Hindu communities. For after all, even among the Hindus, those who travel overseas eat unclean meat. Also the language of all Hindus is not the same. Nor is it true that they all believe in the same deity. In other words, even among those who are properly counted as a part of Hindu society, local customs and folk customs vary so much that there is no reason not to regard the Juangs as a non-Aryan community belonging to the Hindu fold.'[30]

---

[30] Bose, *Hindu Samajer Garhan*, op. cit., p. 14.

In speaking about the Chota Nagpur tribes Bose emphasized two facts: (i) the many similarities in custom between 'tribes' and 'castes' and (ii) the many ties of interdependence between them. Bose's argument appears more persuasive in the Bengali language where the same word, *jati*, is freely used to refer to both caste and tribe.

Bailey has taken all these points into account and has made what is probably the only serious attempt in recent times to discriminate between tribe and caste in structural terms. He warns us against the attempt 'to see particular societies disjunctively as *either* tribes *or* castes',[31] and suggests that we view them in terms of a continuum. Further, he seeks to make the distinction not in terms of the totality of behaviour but, in a more limited way, in relation to the politico-economic system, which corresponds closely to the context of this discussion. Briefly, Bailey's argument is that a caste society is 'organic' and hierarchical while a tribal society is 'segmentary' and egalitarian. He points to the fact that in the Kondmals, which he takes as an example, the relation to the land was very different among the Konds as compared to the Oriyas. About the Konds he says: 'Membership of the clan is, under the system, a condition of holding and exploiting land in the clan territory. A right to land is not achieved by subordination to anyone else, but by equality as a kinsman.'[32] In the Oriya case the right to the use of land is achieved by subordination to the members of the dominant caste. If this is the case then Kond and Oriya peasants are of two different kinds.

But we must remember that the Konds have been shifting cultivators in the very recent past and that even at the time of Bailey's fieldwork they combined axe cultivation with plough cultivation. In considering the larger Chota Nagpur tribes like the Santals, Oraons, Mundas and Hos who have lived as settled agriculturists for a long time, we will find that the territorial identity of the clan, the corporate character of the lineage and the equality among kinsmen have ceased to be effective for a long time. If we go back to Bose's account of the Mundas referred to earlier, we will find that structurally they were ceasing to be a tribe already in the eighteenth century. Bailey himself clearly sees the limited practical value of his scheme in contemporary India where both caste and tribe are becoming rapidly transformed. He tells us at the end of his analysis that 'both caste and tribe are being merged into a different system

---

[31] Bailey, ' "Tribe" and "Caste" in India', op.cit., p. 15.
[32] Ibid., pp. 11–12.

which is neither one nor the other'.[33] This is an agrarian system whose base consists of a heterogeneous body of peasants cut up into various ethno-linguistic categories.

APPENDIX
On the Concept of Tribe

The Constitution of India gives recognition to a category of people designated as the Scheduled Tribes, and makes special provisions for their political representation and their economic and social welfare. The Scheduled Tribes and the Scheduled Castes constitute the two principal components of the backward classes towards which the Government of India has adopted a policy of protective discrimination. This policy has various implications, and questions are raised from time to time about the exact basis of the social identity of the communities whose members are its beneficiaries. These matters come up before the courts, and some lawyers at least seem to assume that there must be a clear answer to the question as to what constitutes a tribe within the knowledge of the sociologist or the social anthropologist.

Anthropologists have since the time of Lewis Henry Morgan argued about the definition of tribe, but very little account has been taken of the tribal communities of India in these general debates over definition. This is unfortunate, not only because of the legal and constitutional significance of the problem, but also because of the size and variety of the tribal population of India. This population comprises about 6.5 per cent of the total, and stood at nearly 40 million at the 1971 census. There are said to be over 400 tribes in India, and they cover the widest range of variation in terms of race, religion and language, as well as economic and political organization.

It is sometimes said that in putting the policy of protective discrimination into action officials of the Government of India are interested not in tribes as such but in only those communities that have been identified and listed as the Scheduled Tribes. But this is to evade the issue, for it can hardly be maintained that the list itself is a random collection of communities put together with no regard for any rational criteria of classification. As a matter of fact, the criteria used have been several and varied; they have not always been related to each other; and they have been left implicit more often than made explicit.

The list of Scheduled Tribes now in use has been constructed by the efforts of various people, beginning more than a hundred years ago. The British Indian civil servants of the nineteenth century often combined the duties of administration with the pleasures of ethnography. Their labours produced a large corpus of reports, manuals and gazetteers devoted to the enumeration and description of the peoples of India. The decennial census provided these ethnographer-administrators with opportunities for constructing a kind of ethnographic map of India, which they hoped to use in the administration of the country. They proceeded by trial and error, rather than according to any clearly formulated system of classification.

---

[33] Ibid., p. 18.

The earlier accounts of the peoples of India show a preoccupation with the identification and description of the various tribes and castes in the population, without any clear criterion of distinction between the two kinds of units. What are now acknowledged as castes are freely described as tribes, and vice versa. Even today it is not always easy to tell whether a particular group should be described as a caste or a tribe. Yet it might seem that if only we followed the anthropologist's definition of 'tribe' nothing would be easier than to distinguish between the two. In practice the distinction between 'tribe' and 'caste' continues to bedevil the student of Indian society, and so we must ask whether this does not reveal a deficiency in the conception itself of tribe.

Anthropological convention has treated the tribe as a 'completely organized society',[1] i.e. a self-perpetuating system having within its boundaries all the resources necessary for the continued maintenance of a particular mode of collective existence. The tribe is in this sense a whole society and a whole culture, unlike the moiety, the phratry, the clan, the lineage or the family. Each tribe has its own territory, which means that it is politically autonomous, whether or not it is politically organized. It also has its own language or dialect which is the mark of its distinctive culture. It has been tacitly assumed that, as in the case of the nation-states of Europe, common territory and common language go hand in hand.

Until recently social anthropologists have been inclined to take the boundaries of the tribe for granted, focusing their attention on its internal structure. It is as if a tribe could be understood on its own terms without taking into account other tribes or other societies of a different kind. The work of Evans-Pritchard among the Nuer showed that a tribe is a tribe only in opposition to other tribes.[2] The experience of India (and other Asian societies) would seem to indicate that a tribe might usefully be viewed as a tribe only in opposition to a social order of another kind.

Nineteenth-century scholars viewed tribal societies in the light of evolutionary theory. This was true not only of anthropologists like Lewis Henry Morgan but also of historians like Fustel de Coulanges. Morgan sought to demonstrate the stages of social evolution by the comparison of contemporary primitive societies. Fustel reconstructed the transformation of Greek and Roman society from a primitive to an advanced type. In all of this the tribe represented a type of social organization as well as a stage in social evolution.

The evolutionary perspective has been revived in the writings of Marshall Sahlins and in Godelier's critique of Sahlins.[3] Godelier goes back to the writings of Morgan to argue that we can understand the tribe as a type of social organization only if we view it as a stage in social evolution. Now, we may follow Morgan and show how savagery is replaced by barbarism which in turn is replaced by civilization; or we may use a more differentiated sequence of stages, identifying the tribal type of organization with a particular stage in the sequence. But the real problem, it seems to me, lies not in identifying the evolutionary stage to which the tribal type of organization corresponds, but in coming to terms with the coexistence of the tribal and other types of organization within the same social and historical context. And it is precisely here that the evolutionists of both the past and the present fail to give satisfaction, in so far as evolutionary theory cannot be a substitute for historical understanding.

The trouble with nineteenth-century evolutionists was that they too readily believed that the development of a more complex or a more advanced type of society led automatically to the effacement of the tribal type. It is a truism that tribe has preceded state and civilization on the broad scale of social evolution. That is not the problem. The problem is that tribes have for centuries and millennia continued to exist on the lap of state and civilization, and to be marked by their impress. The evolutionist is preoccupied with the succession of types; our problem is how to deal with the coexistence of types in the multi-structural formations that are a characteristic feature of so many Asian societies.

Godelier has drawn attention to the two schemes of classification presented by Sahlins in his discussion of tribes. In the first scheme, presented in 1961, there are four types of organization corresponding to four stages of evolution: the band, the tribe, the chiefdom and the state. In a longer essay, published seven years later, the scheme is somewhat simplified, and, instead of four, we have three types, namely, the band, the tribe and the state. Godelier finds fault with Sahlins for collapsing the two middle terms of his first scheme (tribe and chiefdom) into one, and so making his later conception of tribe somewhat more elastic than his earlier.

In his first essay Sahlins had considered a segmentary structure to be the defining feature of the tribe as a type of society. The significance of segmentary political systems was brought to light by British social anthropologists who had worked in Africa. The initial effect of the publication of *African Political Systems* was to highlight the differences between centralized and segmentary societies, characterized by Fortes and Evans-Pritchard as societies of Group A and Group B. However, it soon became apparent that the distinction between the tribe as segmentary system and the tribe as chiefdom is relative rather than absolute. In the interval between the first and the second essays by Sahlins, Gluckman had published his authoritative work in which he had argued that 'the difference between tribes organized under chiefs and those which lack chiefs is not as great as it appears to be'.[4] Even such a redoubtable ethnographer as Malinowski had, it would seem, mistaken for a chiefdom a system that was basically segmentary in character.[5]

In the hundred years since Morgan anthropologists have learnt to distinguish analytically between the band, the segmentary system and the chiefdom. But they have continued, by and large, to apply the same term 'tribe' to all the three. It is to some extent a matter of convenience whether we emphasize the continuities between the three modes of tribal organization or their discontinuities. For those who are interested in examining as a historical process the interactions between tribe and state (or between tribe and civilization) there are obvious advantages in starting with the continuities between the various modes of tribal organization.

The several hundred units that comprise the Scheduled Tribes of India cover all the modes of tribal organization from the band to the chiefdom. This was so as far back as the early nineteenth century when the tribal areas began to be systematically opened up by the colonial administration. Indeed, up to that period one might with some justice speak of 'tribal states' in addition to tribal bands, segmentary tribes and tribal chiefdoms. Historically, whether a given tribe was to be reckoned as a tribal chiefdom or qualified as a tribal state depended very much on the fluctuating fortunes of the larger polity of which it was a part or to which it was related, and not simply on its own evolutionary potential.

At the beginning of the nineteenth century the mix of the different modes of tribal organization among those who comprise the Scheduled Tribes of today was different from the present mix. Bands of hunters and gatherers such as still exist among the Andaman Islanders, or, on the mainland, among the Birhors, were more common then than now. The segmentary mode of tribal organization was also more common in Orissa, Madhya Pradesh, Bihar and in the frontier areas. But there were chiefdoms as well, in addition to the tribal states referred to above.

The concept of tribe thus faces a double problem in the context of Indian society. There is first of all the problem of discriminating among related and overlapping modes of tribal organization. There is the equally vexatious problem of drawing clear lines of demarcation between tribal and non-tribal society. In a sense the first problem is only an aspect of the second.

In North America, Australia, Melanesia, Polynesia and, to a large extent, even in Africa south of the Sahara, the relationship between tribe and civilization (or between tribe and state) has been of a very different order from this relationship in India and in Asian countries generally. It is for this reason that a concept of tribe based on the experience of Australia or North America—the richest fields of classical anthropology—can do little justice to the realities of the Indian situation. In India evolutionary schemes which outline the succession of different types of social organisation must yield to the actual historical analysis of coexisting social formations varying widely in scale and complexity.

In North America, in Melanesia and in Australia the encounter between tribe and civilization was sharp and sudden; and it has a dramatic, not to say traumatic, character. The conditions of the encounter were such as to bring out the contrast and the cleavage between tribe and civilization, rather than the overlap and the continuity between them. Australia provides the best example: here tribe and civilization represented the two extremes on the scales of technology, social organization and ideology. Race, language and culture divided the tribal from the non-tribal population so sharply that there never could be, as in India, any doubt about their respective identities.

In India the encounters between tribe and civilization have taken place under historical conditions of a radically different sort. The coexistence of tribe and civilization, and their mutual interaction go back to the beginnings of recorded history and earlier. Tribes have existed at the margins of Hindu civilization from time immemorial, and these margins have always been vague, uncertain and fluctuating.[6] Hindu civilization acknowledged the distinction between tribe and caste in the distinction between two kinds of communities, *jana* and *jati*, the one confined to the isolation of hills and forests, the other settled in villages and towns with a more elaborate division of labour. The transformation of tribes into castes has been documented by a large number of anthropologists and historians; undoubtedly, the opposite process also took place, though it cannot be as easily documented.

The tribe as a mode of organization has always differed from the caste-based mode of organization. But considered as individual units, tribes are not always easy to distinguish from castes, particularly at the margins where the two modes of organization meet. The native terminology itself reflects this ambiguity. For instance, in the Bengali language the term for caste is *jati* and the term for tribe is *upajati*; but *upajati* might also denote subcaste.

The distinctive condition of the tribe in India has been its isolation, mainly in the interior hills and forests, but also in the frontier regions. By and large the tribal communities are those which were either left behind in these ecological niches or pushed back into them in course of the expansion of state and civilization. Their material culture and their social organization have largely been related to the ecological niches in which they have lived their isolated lives.

The isolation of the tribal communities is and always has been a matter of degree. Some tribes have been more isolated than others, but at least in the interior areas, where the bulk of the tribal population is to be found, none has been completely free from the impress of the wider civilization. Their isolation, whether self-imposed or imposed by others, blocked the growth of their material culture, but it also enabled them to retain their distinctive modes of speech. Today, the most important single indicator of the distinction between tribe and caste is language. The castes speak one or another of the major literary languages; each tribe has its own distinctive dialect which might differ fundamentally from the prevalent regional language. But even this test of identity does not always work. There are many tribes in western India, including the Bhils, one of the most populous in the country, who do not have any language of their own, having at an unknown date adopted the language of the region. It is no accident that from time immemorial the Bhils have also been associated, both materially and symbolically, with some of the most important states in the history of western India.

NOTES

[1] This is Morgan's phrase, repeated in a recent text by Godelier referred to in note 3, below.

[2] E. E. Evans-Pritchard, *The Nuer*, Clarendon Press, 1940; see also M. Fortes and E. E. Evans-Pritchard (eds.), *African Political Systems*, Oxford University Press, 1940.

[3] Marshall D. Sahlins, 'The Segmentary Lineage: and Organization of Predatory Expansion', *American Anthropologist*, Vol. 63, 1961, pp. 322–45; Marshall D. Sahlins, *Tribesmen*, Prentice Hall, 1968; Maurice Godelier, *Perspectives in Marxist Anthropology*, Cambridge University Press, 1977.

[4] Max Gluckman, *Politics, Law and Ritual in Tribal Society*, p. 85, Basil Blackwell, 1965.

[5] J. P. Singh Uberoi, *The Politics of the Kula Ring*, Manchester University Press, 1962.

[6] There is a vast literature on the subject, but the best single account is in N. K. Bose, *The Structure of Hindu Society*, Orient Longman, 1975.

5
Peasants and Workers

APART FROM academic anthropology, the tradition of Marxian inquiry has contributed much to our understanding of the peasantry. Whereas anthropologists began by viewing peasants in opposition to tribesmen, for Marxists the fundamental problem has been, and continues to be, the position of peasants in relation to workers. These two different points of departure are rooted in divergent conceptions of the relation between thought and action, and they have led to different perspectives on the peasant question. Taken together they tell us much about the nature of agrarian social structure.

There are certain striking similarities between the two approaches to the problem. Both have what may be very broadly described as an evolutionary orientation. The anthropologist not only views tribe and peasantry as two different modes of organization but sees the transformtion of the one into the other as a general if not universal process. Similarly, for the Marxist, where peasants and workers co-exist in the same society, they represent two different types of socio-economic formation, one more advanced than the other.

The academic anthropologist tends to view the transformation of tribe into peasantry as a kind of natural process of development. the Marxist, on the other hand, views the transformation of peasants into workers as both a natural process and an object of political action.

The question of when and how tribesmen become peasants has been in the main an academic one. But the transformation of peasants into workers and the role of peasants and workers in the general transformation of society have been as much political as academic questions. Whether one views the social situation and economic interests of peasants and of workers as being fundamentally the same or fundamentally different depends in some measure on one's political orientations. For this reason it is not always easy to achieve clarity about the conditions of these two strata in society and their mutual relations.

The so-called dynamic conception of society is often used as a double-edged weapon. It may be used to argue that the position of peasants and of workers is the same or that it is not the same. If one chooses one can show that the interests of the two are in conflict at any given point of time. But this can be reconciled with the view that over a period of time their interests will become convergent. The absence of a universally acceptable theory of social change makes it difficult for those who are not partisans to determine the actual alignment of groups and their interests in a particular society.

It is well known that on the whole Marx himself adopted a dismissive attitude in regard to the peasantry. This has to be understood in the light of his general theory of social change and his specific interest in the transformation of capitalism into socialism. In Marx's scheme of analysis this transformation was to be spearheaded by the industrial working class. The peasantry represented not the vanguard of the new social order but the residue of the old. The centre of the political arena was to be taken up by the conflict between capitalists and workers; the peasants would at best occupy the sidelines.

Lenin's attitude towards the peasantry was manifestly different. He wrote much more about them and clearly saw them playing a more significant role in social transformation than did Marx. We must remember that Marx was writing primarily about countries like France, Germany and England. Lenin, on the other hand, always had Russia at the centre of his mind, and Russia was a backward country with a massive population of peasants. As one who was involved directly in the organization of a major political programme in a predominantly agrarian society, Lenin could not afford to adopt a dismissive attitude towards the peasantry.

In his writings on the peasantry Lenin sought to make consistent use of the Marxian tools of analysis. For although he conceded that many differences prevailed between peasants and workers, he argued that they were both coming increasingly under the influence of the capitalist economic system. This in his view was leading to a steady convergence between the vast majority of peasants and the industrial workers in the economic and political fields. As is well known, he drew much on Kautsky's study of conditions in Germany in elaborating his own arguments, although there were certain basic differences between the two points of view.

Although Lenin attached much greater significance to the peasantry than did Marx, he too believed that it was the industrial worker who would constitute the vanguard of the new social order. The peasants were to play their historic role by aligning themselves with the working class movement since the interests of the two were convergent; the task of social analysis was to demonstrate by a careful collection of data that this convergence was in fact bringing the two closer together. It is only with Mao Tse-tung and the success of the Chinese Communist movement that the peasants are brought to the centre of the historical arena. However much one might argue about the continuity of thought between Marx and Mao, no two thinkers could differ more profoundly on their assessment of the social and historical significance of the peasantry.

The success of peasant movements in China and elsewhere in the Third World has created a new image of the peasantry. A hundred years ago peasants were considered to be quintessentially backward and conservative. Today they have come to be regarded by some as having great potential for revolutionary change. Unfortunately, the revolutionary potential of the peasantry (or of any social stratum) in a country comes to be widely appreciated only after some dramatic change has taken place in its fortunes. But the task of the sociologist is not so much to speculate on what might happen or on what might have happened, as to discuss objectively the prevailing alignment of groups and categories in a society.

In discussing peasants and workers we are dealing with the system of stratification of a society or with its class structure. Some scholars would distinguish between stratification and class by saying that the former refers to the gradation of groups in a society while the latter refers to the conflict of interests between them.[1] Even though it may be possible to distinguish between the two analytically, there is in reality a great deal of convergence between them. We shall discuss not only the place of the peasantry in the scheme of social gradation but also the conflict or identity of interests between them and other social categories.

[1] Georges Gurvitch and Ralf Dahrendorf are two among many European sociologists who have argued in this way. For a brief discussion of their point of view, see my 'Ideas and Interests' in *Studies in Agrarian Social Structure*, O.U.P., 1973.

From the sociological point of view the great merit of Lenin's work was that he did not take the peasants to be a homogeneous or undifferentiated category, but devoted himself to a serious examination of their internal structure.[2] His was very different from the view that peasants were 'like potatoes in a sack of potatoes'[3] or that they were a community of equals bound by organic ties to each other and to the land. Marx too contrasts two types of peasants, the revolutionary and enlightened peasant who looks to the future, and the conservative and superstitious peasant who looks to the past; but this contrast serves more the purpose of polemic than of scientific analysis.

As Ossowski[4] has pointed out, Lenin's subdivision of the Russian peasantry into *kulak* (or rich peasant), *stredniak* (or middle peasant) and *bedniak* (or poor peasant) has provided students of the peasantry with a conceptual scheme which is of general significance. While his ultimate aim might have been to predict and direct the political orientations of the different subdivisions in terms of a pre-existing theory of ideology, he took great pains to analyse the social and economic characteristics of each one of them.

Lenin's views on the Russian peasantry were developed in opposition to those of the *narodniki*.[5] The latter were champions of the traditional Russian *mir* which in their view was a natural, organic community of equals. They sought to resist the onslaught of external forces which might threaten the unity and harmony of the *mir*. Lenin argued that their view of the Russian *mir* was idyllic and that it bore little correspondence with existing realities. It was in this context that he relentlessly exposed the inequalities and contradictions within the peasantry itself. In his view an ideology which glorified the peasantry as a whole must inevitably justify the exploitation of the poor peasant by the rich.

Lenin's analyses of the Russian peasantry should make us cautious about accepting a blanket characterization of peasants being subjected to 'domination by outsiders'. For it is clear that whatever the position might have been in the past, the rich peasants about whom Lenin spoke did not necessarily occupy an underdog position, and

[2] See V. I. Lenin, *Selected Works*, Vol. XII, International Publishers, 1943, and in it particularly 'The Agrarian Question and the "Critics of Marx" '; also his *To The Rural Poor*, Progress Publishers, 1967.

[3] This is a paraphrase of Marx's well-known statement in his *The Eighteenth Brumaire of Louis Bonaparte*, Foreign Languages Publishing House, n.d.

[4] Stanislav Ossowski, *Class Structure in the Social Consciousness*, Routledge and Kegan Paul, 1963, p. 44 n.

[5] See Lenin, *Selected Works*, op. cit.

the poor peasants were not subjected to domination only by outsiders. It is possible that Lenin exaggerated the cleavage between the rich peasants and the rural poor for reasons of polemic, but the cleavage itself could not have been his invention.

If we turn to rural society in India we will find not only inequalities between groups but also conflicts of interests between them. These inequalities and conflicts are centred in an important way around the ownership, control and use of land. In very general terms the agricultural population of India may be divided into three categories. These are (i) non-cultivating owners and tenure holders; (ii) owner-cultivators and cultivating tenants with recognized rights of tenancy; and (iii) share-croppers and agricultural labourers. In the strict sense of the term only those belonging to category (ii) are peasants; members of categories (ii) and (iii) together may be called peasants in a loose way; those belonging to category (i) cannot be described as peasants in any sense of the term.

Indian sociologists have grown accustomed to viewing the social hierarchy in terms of caste where the categories are mutually exclusive and are divided by boundaries which are sharp and clearly defined. They are inclined to be a little baffled when confronted with categories which are indefinite, ill-defined and frequently overlapping. If one has a neat and tidy mind one will find it enormously more satisfying to talk about Rajputs, Jats and Chamars than about landlords, peasants and agricultural labourers.

The difficulties in demarcating clearly the categories with which we are concerned should be emphasized. The threefold division of the peasantry by Lenin into *kulak*, *stredniak* and *bedniak* probably represented cleavages generally recognized by the people themselves so that even if the divisions cannot be precisely delimited, there is a good sociological reason for starting one's analyses with them. But what is misleading is to assume that divisions of exactly the same kind provide significant cleavages in every type of agrarian society. In the Indian case we may need a twofold or a fourfold division, or a threefold division of a somewhat different kind. The spirit of Marxian inquiry does not require that students of rural society in India should imitate in every detail the scheme adopted by Lenin for the study of rural society in Russia.

From what has been said earlier it should be evident that the category 'peasant' is not always found in its pure form in India. It merges with the non-working landowner at one end and the landless agricultural worker at the other. This kind of overlap may be observed not only in the 'peasant' community and the 'peasant' caste but also in the peasant household if we examine it over a period of time. It is caused partly by the very sensitive inverse relation between manual work and high social status, and partly by the extreme fragmentation of landholdings.

A peasant household, in the strict sense of the term, is a household in which both men and women perform the bulk of the agricultural work on land which they themselves either own or effectively control. In India, particularly in areas of wet paddy cultivation, there has been a marked tendency for first women and then men to withdraw from agricultural work as soon as economic circumstances make it possible. When this withdrawal is complete and the land is worked by either sharecroppers or agricultural labourers, the household is no longer a peasant household but one of landowners. But the withdrawal rarely takes place in one decisive step so that there are all kinds of intermediate stages between a purely peasant household and a household of non-working landowners.

At the other end of the scale, the extreme fragmentation of holdings makes the peasant depend less and less on his own land, and more and more on work as either wage labourer or sharecropper on land owned and controlled by others. Here also there is rarely a sharp break which makes the household become solely dependent on wage labour, and there are all kinds of transitional stages between the poor peasant and the pure agricultural worker.

A word of caution needs to be introduced at this stage. The processes of increasing withdrawal from manual work and increasing dependence on wage employment appear as processes of change from the viewpoint of the individual actors involved. But they may or may not represent a change in the social system taken as a whole. There is every reason to believe that a certain amount of circulation of individuals between the kinds of roles we are considering was a normal feature of the traditional system. While this circulation has undoubtedly increased in recent times, we do not have any exact measure of either the extent or the significance of this increase.

Thus, those whom we may properly designate as peasants in India are not a clearly-defined type, but a category whose edges become easily blurred. This category, which appears as a unity in opposition to landowners, is itself internally differentiated. What is the best way of representing this internal differentiation? Before we decide to employ such blanket phrases as 'rich', 'middle' and 'poor' it may be worthwhile to enquire what they signify in terms of the structure of social relations.

Clearly, the meanings that we attach to phrases like 'rich', 'middle' and 'poor' will vary not only from one region to another but also from one point of time to another. One obvious way of differentiating between peasants is by the size of their holdings; this provides a way of classifying them according to information that is relatively easy to obtain. But there are obvious limitations in this. The productivity of land varies greatly not only from one region to another but between holdings within the same village. Further, differences in tenurial status must be taken into account; operational holdings of the same size might vary greatly in their proportions of land owned to land leased in.

In addition to the size of holding one might take into account other assets such as livestock and farm machinery. Lenin believed that the amount of livestock, particularly horses, owned gave an accurate indication of the economic position of a peasant household.[6] It would be difficult to say how far this is true in India in regard to plough cattle, for it is not uncommon for even poor peasants to own plough cattle along with which they hire themselves out for wages on land owned by wealthier people. The use of farm machinery is as yet uncommon for the country as a whole, and machinery is probably most widely used by those who are more properly described as farmers rather than peasants.

Variations in the size, status and quality of holdings, and in the nature and amount of other agricultural assets govern variations of household income among the peasantry. Even if we ignore for the time being the difficulties inherent in computing agricultural income, a subdivision of the peasantry (or of any social stratum) in terms of income will remain in some sense arbitrary. For where there is a continuous distribution of income within a certain range, there are no natural cutting-off points by which we can decide whether there should be two, three or four subdivisions and what these should be.[7]

---

[6] Ibid.

[7] For a general discussion of this problem, see Stanislav Ossowski, 'Old Notions and New Problems: Interpretations of Social Structure in Modern Society' in André Béteille (ed.), *Social Inequality*, Penguin, 1969; for a discussion relating to the agrarian social structure in an Indian state, see my 'Class Structure in an Agrarian Society' in *Studies in Agrarian Social Structure*, op. cit.

An equally good if not a better way of classifying peasants is in terms of their degree of participation in the actual work of agriculture. I said that a peasant household, ideally conceived, is one whose members themselves cultivate their land and neither hire in workers from outside nor hire themselves out to work for others. But this ideal is rarely if ever fully met. Peasant households hire workers in for specific activities and peasants hire themselves out seasonally without necessarily losing the basic characteristics by which they are defined. Indeed it is not uncommon for the same household both to hire in and to hire out workers in return for wages.

Thus, using the criterion of hired work, it may be possible to classify peasants into three broad categories. Firstly, there are those who regularly depend on hired hands to supplement the labour contributed by members of the household. Secondly, there are those who regularly work for others in addition to cultivating the land which they themselves own or control. Lastly, there are those who do not hire others to work for them or hire themselves out to work for others, as well as those who do a little of both. As in the case of divisions by size of holding or income, although to a lesser extent, the cutting-off points here also may have to be arbitrarily chosen.

There will no doubt be a broad correspondence between the classification of peasants according to their size of holding (or income) and their classification according to the degree and extent of participation in work. But it will be misleading to treat the two classifications as interchangeable on the assumption that whether people engage hired workers and whether they hire themselves out for work depend solely on their economic condition. In fact the extent to which the two classifications—by size of holding and by participation in work—correspond itself differs appreciably from one culture to another.

In India peasant households which are of high social status (or believe themselves to be of high social status) generally discourage their women from working in the fields and may therefore be obliged to hire workers regularly for particular agricultural operations even when their holdings are of small size. On the other hand, in households where there is tradition for both men and women to do agricultural work, there may be less dependence on hired workers even when the holdings are fairly large. There is a close relationship in India between the presence of a large body of agricultural workers and the elaborate social gradation of the different types of agricultural work, and this gradation itself is not governed solely by material considerations.

In characterizing the peasantry I have emphasized all along the fact of their direct participation in manual work. Not all peasants participate in work to the same extent. There are important differences in the type of work they do according to age and sex. Some peasants hire workers more or less regularly to supplement the work done by members of the household. But participation in manual work in one form or another is a universal feature of all peasant households. From this point of view the peasantry are fundamentally different from the gentry, and there is a basic similarity between peasants and workers.

Do peasants and workers constitute a single class? Lenin raised this question and answered it categorically in the negative.[8] Peasants and industrial workers may be contrasted in a variety of ways. There are differences in their economic condition, their cultural life and their political orientation. As is well known, Marx was not prepared to regard the French peasantry of the mid-nineteenth century as a class since they lacked political consciousness and organization.[9] Do peasants become a class by the mere creation of a political association which claims to represent their interests? How does one assess the level of political consciousness among the peasantry?

Both Marx and Lenin used industrial workers as a yardstick for assessing 'class-formation' among the peasantry, and we certainly deepen our insight into the latter by viewing them alongside the former. One important difference between the two is that industrial workers are a much more clearly delimited category than peasants. The pure industrial worker is much more easy to identify than the pure peasant, particularly in a country like India with its complex tenurial history, its extreme fragmentation of holdings and its elaborate gradation of the different types of traditional manual work.

The characteristics of the Indian peasantry as a stratum (or a class) and their position vis-à-vis the workers may be considered in terms of various criteria. Let us consider them in terms of the

[8] V. I. Lenin, 'The Peasantry and the Working Class' in *Selected Works*, Vol. XII, op. cit.
[9] Marx, *The Eighteenth Brumaire*, op. cit.

following: (i) market situation; (ii) work situation; (iii) status situation; and (iv) political situation. At this stage of our enquiry only a brief indication can be given of the kinds of questions that require to be answered.

The market situation is, in David Lockwood's terms, 'the economic position narrowly conceived, consisting of source and size of income, degree of job-security, and opportunity for upward mobility'.[10] Clearly the market situations of peasants and of industrial workers are very different. The peasant is an own-account worker who controls his means of production while the industrial worker is an employee, working with instruments owned and controlled by others. Even when the peasant's income becomes increasingly responsive to market forces, it is never responsive to them in the same way as the worker's income. Further, the upward mobility of peasants (from 'poor' to 'middle' or from 'middle' to 'rich') is governed by forces which are very different from those which govern upward mobility among industrial workers; the same is of course true of downward mobility.

A point that has been recognized by authorities from Marx to Lenin is that it is in regard to economic security that peasants differ most characteristically from industrial workers. It is not as if the economic security of peasants (and particularly of small-holding peasants) is never threatened by market forces. But the impact of these forces and the time-scale over which they operate are different in the two cases, so that peasants and workers have often diametrically opposed views of what constitutes a threat to their economic security.

The work situation refers to 'the set of social relationships in which the individual is involved at work by virtue of his position in the division of labour'.[11] Marx has described the work situation of the French peasantry in characteristic terms.[12] Put in a nutshell, his argument is that the work situation of the peasant isolates him from other peasants whereas the work situation of the industrial worker brings him increasingly closer to other industrial workers.

To the extent that the family farm is the basic unit of economic organization among the peasantry, the domestic group provides the basic framework for most of the effective relations involving work;

[10] David Lockwood, *The Blackcoated Worker*, Allen and Unwin, 1958, p. 15.
[11] Ibid., p. 15.
[12] Marx, *The Eighteenth Brumaire*, op. cit.

the division of labour is governed primarily by the age and sex composition of the household. Relations involving work which extend beyond the domestic group are in the case of peasants generally confined within the local community. In the case of industrial workers, the work situation involves relations which are detached not only from the domestic context, but also to a large extent from the context of the local community.

The status situation of a class or a stratum refers to the prestige enjoyed by its members. There are major difficulties in comparing peasants with industrial workers from this point of view. For while there is an elaborate gradation of work in Indian society, there is no obvious way in which traditional types of work can be compared with those of more recent origin.

Even if one were to have a single prestige rating of the various activities in agriculture and in industry, one would still have problems of comparability. For in assessing the status situation of a stratum we have to consider not only the work performed by its members but also the degree of independence enjoyed by them in their work. Industrial activities might be rated higher than agricultural, but being an own-account worker rather than an employee might more than offset the negative value placed on agricultural work.

The political situation of a stratum or a class is to be viewed in the light of the level of political consciousness among its members and the existence of movements and associations to give expression to this consciousness in the political arena. In terms of Marx's famous dictum, a stratum does not become a class so long as there is 'merely a local interconnexion' among its members and 'the identity of their interests begets no community, no national bond and no political organization among them'.[13]

I have considered the political situation as a factor in its own right because although it clearly is affected by the market situation, the work situation and the status situation, it affects all these factors in its turn. Thus, it is well known that where there is an effective political organization among workers, they may alter their market situation as well as their work situation to their advantage.

Thus, it is not enough to say that peasants—like industrial workers—occupy an underdog position and are subjected to exploitation. Not only the manner of their exploitation but also their

[13] Ibid., p. 124.

response to it may be different. Further, the possibilities of organizing peasant movements and associations have altered vastly since Marx wrote about the French peasantry more than a hundred years ago, and there is no reason to believe as Lenin seems to have believed that such movements or associations must necessarily depend for their leadership on the organized industrial working class. How peasants will respond to their political situation cannot be determined in terms of some pre-existing general theory but will have to be established empirically for each type of society.

So far we have viewed peasants in relation to industrial workers. These are strata or classes which may be compared and contrasted but which do not interact with each other directly. In my view it is more fruitful to see peasants in relation to agricultural workers, for here we may consider not only similarities and differences but also direct interaction between the two.

There is a question of terminology which needs to be settled first of all. As Daniel Thorner has pointed out, the term 'peasant' may be used in a broad as well as a narrow sense.[14] In the narrow sense 'peasants' are smallholders who live by cultivating land which they themselves own or control. But in the broad sense, which is very commonly adopted, 'peasants' are all those who live by working on the land including sharecroppers and agricultural workers. The Marxists have more or less consistently used the word in its more narrow and rigorous meaning, and I propose to follow their usage because it is only in this way that we can explore more deeply the relationship between those who work on land they themselves control and those who work on land controlled by others.

While accepting the more rigorous definition of peasantry and the distinction implicit in it between peasants and agricultural workers, we must keep in mind the reason why the broader conception is so commonly used. For although it is both possible and desirable to make the distinction analytically, in the real world there is frequent and considerable overlap between the two categories. This has significant implications for the relations between peasants and agricultural workers. Where there is much overlap between the two categories, the relations between peasants and agricultural

[14] Daniel Thorner, 'Peasantry' in David L. Sils (ed.), *International Encyclopedia of the Social Sciences*, The MacMillan Company and The Free Press, 1968, pp. 503–11.

workers are of one kind; where the overlap is reduced and the categories become mutually exclusive, the relations are of a different kind.

India has a large population of agricultural workers. This population has grown both absolutely and relatively to the other agrarian strata over the last century, and probably with increasing rapidity over the last decade. But it has been established beyond reasonable doubt that there was a considerable population of agricultural workers at the beginning of the nineteenth century,[15] so that those who worked on the land were not a homogeneous category even at the inception of British rule.

The term 'agricultural worker' can no doubt be used narrowly to refer only to those who work for wages in cash and are bound to their employers by the cash nexus. Agricultural workers in this sense are probably of relatively recent origin, but it would be unduly restrictive to use the term in this way and to exclude workers who are paid in kind or are bound to their masters by traditional obligations. For there is much historical as well as sociological continuity between agricultural workers who are paid in cash and those who are paid in kind.

Almost exactly 30 per cent of the total workers and a little under 40 per cent of the workers in agriculture were recorded as being agricultural labourers at the 1971 census. These aggregate figures give only a very broad idea of the density and significance of agricultural labourers in the total work force. In two states, Andhra Pradesh and Kerala, agricultural labourers outnumbered cultivators or constituted more than half the total work force in agriculture, and in two others, Tamil Nadu and Bihar, there were nearly as many agricultural labourers as cultivators.

The figures given in the provisional tables of the 1971 census will have to be treated with some caution for they show some puzzling features which are not very easy to account for. Between 1961 and 1971 the proportion of agricultural labourers among all workers is shown to have increased from 18.87 to 29.98 per cent. In several states such as the Punjab, Haryana and Rajasthan these proportions have more than doubled. Census figures sometimes show dramatic changes which on closer examination prove to be

---

[15] Dharma Kumar, *Land and Caste in South India*, Cambridge University Press 1965.

illusory.[16] But whatever the case may be, it seems certain that there is not only a large population of agricultural workers in the country but also that it is on the increase.

Some of the problems we face in comparing peasants with industrial workers are easily resolved when we compare them with agricultural workers. The market situation of agricultural workers is almost invariably inferior to that of peasants, probably even in those limited areas where wages have shown a substantial rise due either to increased production as in the Punjab or to organized political action as in Kerala. The transformation of the peasant into an agricultural worker is still the most general indicator of the deterioration of the market situation of the former.

The work situation of agricultural workers may or may not be similar to that of peasants. Where they are employed in their own village on a more or less permanent basis and where members of the household are employed together, their work situation may not differ very much from that of owner-cultivators. But agricultural workers are having increasingly to work on somewhat different terms. Wage employment in agriculture is becoming more contractual, and when this happens, the different members of the household may not be employed together or even in the same village. Even here it might be misleading to characterize agricultural workers as a 'rural proletariat' because important differences continue to exist between their work situation and that of industrial workers.

The status of agricultural workers is unambiguously inferior to that of peasants. While they both do the same general kind of work, those who are employed for wages—whether in cash or in kind—are usually burdened with the more onerous and arduous tasks. It is well known that members of the higher 'peasant' castes, such as Jats, who have lost their land may be prepared to work as tenants but are reluctant to hire themselves out as wage labourers, primarily for reasons of status; and what applies to men applies even more strongly to women.

The political situation of agricultural workers reveals a certain ambiguity. Their 'underdog position' makes it in one sense easy to organize them for programmes of radical change. But their sense

[16] See J. Krishnamurty, 'Working Force in 1971 Census: Some Exercises on Provisional Results', *Economic and Political Weekly*, Vol. VII, No. 3, January 1972, pp. 115–18.

of economic insecurity and social inferiority also makes their organization in another sense peculiarly vulnerable. As in all such cases, the strength or weakness of their organization depends on the character of the class against which it is directed.

The political union of agricultural workers has been successful in certain limited parts of the country. On the whole it has been more successful in the areas of wet paddy cultivation, particularly in some districts of South India such as Alleppey in Kerala and Tanjore in Tamil Nadu. In these districts the most successful agrarian organizations are in fact the Agricultural Workers' Unions rather than the Kisan Sabhas which represent the interests of the peasants in general.

It has been argued by some that agricultural wages show a substantial increase only when agricultural workers have a sufficiently strong political organization to demand successfully this increase. Pranab Bardhan has sought to confirm this argument by a comparative study of agricultural wages in the different parts of the country. According to Bardhan, in Ludhiana district (Punjab), where production increased substantially between 1962–3 and 1967–8, the rise in real wages was small whereas in Alleppey and Palghat districts in Kerala they rose much more in the same period.[17]

T. K. Oommen has examined in detail the factors associated with the rise in the real wages of agricultural workers in Alleppey district.[18] This rise has been attended by widespread and intense agrarian conflict. Among the economic factors responsible for the conflict are a large concentration of landless labourers and the extreme fragmentation of holdings. Even at the 1961 census over half the total workers in agriculture were agricultural labourers, and a more recent survey shows that nearly 90 per cent of the operational holdings are of 2.5 acres or less.[19] Although there is much landlessness and fragmentation of holdings throughout India, these figures must be considered unusually high.

There are two specific features of the economic situation of agricultural workers in Alleppey district which deserve attention. The first is the considerable measure of geographical mobility among them. Oommen tells us, 'Roads and transport and communications

---

[17] Pranab Bardhan, 'Green Revolution and Agricultural Labourers', *Economic and Political Weekly*, Vol. V, Nos. 29–31, July 1970, pp. 1239–46.

[18] T. K. Oommen, 'Agrarian Tension in a Kerala District: An Analysis', *Indian Journal of Industrial Relations*, Vol. 7, No. 2, 1971, pp. 229–68.

[19] Cited in Oommen, op. cit.

are well developed in Alleppey district, and this immensely facilitates the movement of men. It is a common sight during harvest seasons that men and women commute in buses to agricultural fields.'[20] Secondly, the same person is quite frequently an agricultural as well as an industrial worker. Both these features are related to the distinctive ecology of settlements in Kerala where rural-urban differences are in general much weaker than elsewhere in the country.

According to Oommen, 'The first agricultural labour union in Kuttanad was formed in 1939, as a branch of the Travancore Karshaka Thozhilali (agricultural labour) Union (TKTU).'[21] From its inception the TKTU was controlled largely by the Communist Party and, with the split in it 1964, there was a corresponding split in the TKTU into the Kerala in Karshaka Thozhilali Federation controlled by the CPI and the Kerala State Karshaka Thozhilali Union controlled by the CPI(M), the latter emerging as the more powerful organization.

The Kerala Government set up a 'tripartite committee consisting of the representatives of the government, farmers, and agricultural labourers'[22] in July 1957. Since then the representatives of the agricultural labourers have extracted a number of concessions in wages and conditions of work, although their effectiveness here as elsewhere has been weakened considerably by inter-union rivalries. Oommen's analysis shows that the relative success of agricultural workers in Alleppey cannot be explained by any one factor, but owes itself to a combination of various factors which may be individually present elsewhere but usually not in the same combination.

Elsewhere we have discussed in some detail the factors that have contributed to the increasing political strength of agricultural workers in Tanjore district in Tamil Nadu.[23] There also there is a powerful Agricultural Workers' Union controlled by the CPM which has played an important part in bargaining for higher wages at tripartite meetings between representatives of employers, employees and Government. I too have argued, like Oommen, that the success of the Agricultural Workers' Union in Tanjore owes itself to a combination of various factors although these are not exactly the

---

[20] Oommen, op. cit., p. 241.
[21] Ibid., p. 246.   [22] Ibid., p. 251.
[23] 'Agrarian Relations in Tanjore District, South India' in my *Studies in Agrarian Social Structure*, op. cit.

same as those identified by Oommen in his analysis of Alleppey district.

The materials from Alleppey as well as Tanjore bring out one point on which comment is required. In discussing relations between employers and employees in agriculture one talks in a loose way of landlords and landless labourers. The point that I would like to make is that very probably a substantial number of the employers of agricultural labourers in both Alleppey and Tanjore would be better described as peasants than as landlords. For these are areas in which over half the people working in agriculture are agricultural labourers and in which the vast majority of operational holdings—in Alleppey district over 98 per cent—are of less than 5 acres. Clearly, many landless labourers must be employed by people who themselves have dwarf holdings. Granted that pure, self-employed peasants must be somewhat uncommon and that we have to deal rather with those who more or less approximate to the pure type, there must be serious conflicts of interest between 'peasants' and agricultural workers.

The presence of these conflicts and the problems created by them for leaders of peasant movements and associations are clearly revealed when we turn to a different area, i.e. West Bengal. West Bengal has a long tradition of agrarian movements and, along with Kerala, it has had the most powerful Kisan Sabha among all the states in India. But the agricultural workers have failed to unite effectively and they have not been able to raise wages and improve conditions of work through organized political action as in Kerala or in Tanjore district.

There are certain differences in objective conditions between West Bengal on the one hand and Kerala and Tanjore district on the other. West Bengal does not have as large a concentration of agricultural workers as either of the two other areas. But more important than that, the pure agricultural labourer who lives only by working for wages is far less common in West Bengal than in Kerala or in Tanjore district. There is a fairly high degree of overlap between cultivating-owners, sharecroppers and wage labourers in most districts of West Bengal. As a consequence, the employer-employee relationship in agriculture has not assumed the importance in this state that it has in some of the areas in the South.

In West Bengal 'cultivators' and 'agricultural labourers' are not only mixed categories economically, but they are also socially very heterogeneous. Agricultural workers are divided into caste Hindus, Harijans and Adivasis. The distinction between Harijans and Adivasis is quite marked in West Bengal, and is often reflected in the settlement pattern of the village. In Tanjore district those talukas which show a preponderance of agricultural workers also show a preponderance of Harijans within this category. By contrast, the many distinctions of status among agricultural workers in West Bengal act as an obstacle to their effective political organization.

The first major agrarian struggle organized by the Kisan Sabha in Bengal was the Tebhaga movement of 1946–7. This movement sought an increase in the share of the sharecropper from one-half to two-thirds, and other improvements in his economic situation. It was organized by the then united Kisan Sabha of the then undivided Bengal. Sunil Sen, the historian of the Tebhaga movement who himself took a leading part in it, gives us some indication of the dilemmas faced by the Kisan Sabha in Bengal from almost its very inception. 'It seems that the overriding consideration of the Kisan Sabha was to preserve peasant unity, and the emphasis was on those demands which corresponded to the immediate interests of all categories of peasants, so that a broad peasant movement could be built up as part of the developing anti-imperialist movement.'[24] In his own account of the Tebhaga movement, Sen systematically ignores the distinction made since Lenin between 'peasants' and 'agricultural workers', and talks frequently of rich peasants, middle peasants, poor peasants and landless peasants (comprising sharecroppers and agricultural workers). Now it is a moot question as to how far the interests of these categories did in fact converge at the time of the Tebhaga movement in 1946–7.

The Tebhaga movement failed by and large to achieve its objectives. But the demands which it had raised continued to exist. There was massive agrarian unrest in West Bengal again between 1968 and 1970. One important difference between the two movements is that the more recent one was organized while United Front governments dominated by the CPI(M) were in office. It was also on a somewhat larger scale and had a more ambitious programme of demands. But the central issue once again was the general one of land to the tiller and the specific one of better terms for the sharecropper. Further, once again the programme sought to emphasize

[24] Sunil Sen, *Agrarian Struggle in Bengal: 1946–47*, People's Publishing House. 1972, p. 80.

peasant unity and to assume an identity of interests between poor peasants, sharecroppers and agricultural workers.

It is difficult to say what permanent gains were achieved by the Kisan Sabha on behalf of the poor peasants and sharecroppers. But agricultural workers did not gain very much, and agricultural wages in West Bengal remain fairly low as compared to Kerala and many other parts of the country.

Some of the structural reasons which impeded the development of an effective union of agricultural workers in West Bengal have earlier been explained. If one reads the documents of the Bengal (and later West Bengal) Kisan Sabha over the last thirty years, one will be struck by the ambivalent attitude of its leadership towards such a union.[25] In the forties the problem was discussed in great detail, and the general opinion was that such a union would be desirable. One finds the same opinion being expressed in the late sixties and the same lack of action. The contrast between Kerala and West Bengal shows that the situation of agricultural workers cannot improve substantially unless they are effectively organized, and that this organization itself presupposes certain structural conditions which are not universally present.

---

[25] See my 'Peasant Associations and the Agrarian Class Structure' in *Studies in Agrarian Social Structure*, op. cit.

6
Marxism and Modern Sociology

IN INDIA TODAY the academic sociologist who seeks to establish a dialogue with practising Marxists must take the risk of having his fingers burnt. It seems that Marxists are quite happy to have sociologists study caste, kinship and ritual, and to make occasional jibes at the triviality of sociological research. But when the sociologist turns to such subjects as the social organization of production, the agrarian class structure or peasant movements and associations, he becomes at once the object of deep suspicion.

The uneasy relationship in which one finds Marxism and academic sociology in contemporary India is by no means unique. The tension between the two approaches, or the two perspectives is ultimately rooted in two possible ways of relating thought and action. Hence it has a kind of universal character, although it manifests itself differently in different places and times.

It is important to remember that academic sociology (including social anthropology) was introduced into India from Britain and America at a time when there was in these countries an almost complete separation between Marxism and sociology. Certainly in most British and American universities between the two Wars people were inclined to believe that sociology was one thing and Marxism quite another, and there was very little ground on which the two could meet. It has been pointed out earlier how Indian scholars inherited from Britain and America the unfortunate distinction between sociology and social anthropology. It can be argued, though only up to a point, that the prevailing separation between sociology and Marxism in India is an unfortunate by-product of the same inheritance.

European sociology has been on the whole much more responsive to Marxism, and the recent growth of interest in Marxism among Anglo-American sociologists is at least partly due to the increasingly easy availability in English translations of works written originally in French, German and Polish. In talking about Marxism no less than about sociology we must not lose sight of the specificity of national intellectual traditions. Marxism has permeated intellectual debate in the European countries to a far greater extent than in Britain or America, and European thinkers are inclined to be more than a little self-conscious about the special character of their intellectual heritage.

In India we tend to overlook the fact that there has been in Europe a close relationship—whether of affinity or of hostility—between Marxism and sociology. France provides a good example of the varieties of dialogue between the two, partly because of the distinctiveness of its own intellectual tradition and partly because it has been an intellectual home for scholars from so many European countries.

In a long chapter entitled 'The Sociology of Karl Marx', Georges Gurvitch, one of Europe's leading sociologists, wrote, 'The object of this study . . . is to show that Marx was the greatest and the least dogmatic of all the founders of sociology.'[1] Gurvitch did much to attract the attention of academic sociologists to the writings of the young Marx, and to build up through his own writings a dialectical sociology. Gurvitch's colleague at the University of Paris, Professor Raymond Aron, has also grappled with the ideas of Marx during most of his career, but in a different spirit: he has sought relentlessly to expose the dogmas of Marxism and to trace them back to their roots in the writings of Marx.[2]

Between Gurvitch's active enthusiasm for Marx and Aron's equally active critique of Marxism various positions are possible. One is that of Professor Lévi-Strauss who wrote: 'When I was about seventeen I was initiated into Marxism by a young Belgian socialist whom I met on a holiday. . . . Reading Marx was for me all the more enthralling in that I was making my first contact, by way of that

[1] Georges Gurvitch, *La Vocation actuelle de la Sociologie*, Presses Univérsitaire de France, 1963, Vol. II, p. 220.

[2] Raymond Aron, *The Opium of the Intellectuals*, Secker and Warburg, 1957; also his *Main Currents in Sociological Thought*, Penguin, 1968, Vol. 1.

great thinker, with the philosophical current that runs from Kant to Hegel. A whole world was opened to me. My excitement has never cooled: and rarely do I tackle a problem in sociology or ethnology without having first set my mind in motion by reperusal of a page or two from the *18th Brumaire of Louis Bonaparte* or the *Critique of Political Economy*.'[3]

And yet when Lévi-Strauss wrote a brilliant, profound and scholarly article on French sociology[4] he did not feel the need to mention Marx even once or to refer to any of his basic ideas.

Why are so many people instinctively enchanted, as it were, by the idea of Marxism? Why are so many others, in an equally unreasoning way, repelled by it? These are not just abstract or idle questions, but must remain with us while we seek to understand the relationship between Marxism and sociology in India.

What kind of a relationship should one expect in India between Marxism and sociology in the years to come? In the absence of any effective or serious debate between the two, it is inevitable that the problem be posed first in somewhat formal terms. It seems that the relationship between Marxism and sociology can be formulated from three points of view. The first is that Marxism provides the basic framework which can retain its fundamental character while absorbing the more fruitful findings of sociology. The second is that sociology is the basic discipline which must grow by accommodating the empirically testable ideas of Marx and of the more creative adherents of Marxism; this is my own point of view. There is however a third position which denies the very possibility of a Marxist sociology and insists that Marxism and sociology are by their nature irreconcilable.

The clearest expression of the first point of view is to be found in the writings of contemporary Soviet sociologists. As is well known, in the Soviet Union first 'bourgeois' sociology and then sociology pure and simple came under a cloud during the Stalinist regime. The subject has been revived again, and Soviet sociologists have since the mid-fifties presented their point of view at international conferences, and have also made their work increasingly available to the outside world through a fair number of English translations.[5]

---

[3] Claude Lévi-Strauss, *Tristes Tropiques* (English tr.), Atheneum, 1963, p. 61.

[4] Claude Lévi-Strauss, 'French Sociology' in G. Gurvitch and W. E. Moore (eds.), *Twentieth Century Sociology*, The Philosophical Library, 1945.

[5] For a brief survey of Soviet Sociology see Alex Simirenko, *Soviet Sociology*, Routledge and Kegan Paul, 1967.

Soviet sociologists maintain a distinction between Marxist and bourgeois sociology. Osipov has set forward in clear terms the relations between historical materialism, social philosophy and sociology. 'Historical materialism as a science concerns general laws governing the emergence, development and changes of socio-economic formations.'[6] The subject matter of social philosophy is 'the study of the specificity of manifestation of dialectical materialist laws (consciousness and being, transition of quantitative to qualitative changes, etc.) in social life and the discovery of new dialectical aspects in the light of modern social development'.[7] Sociology, as one of the specific social sciences, is assigned a more limited sphere. Sociologists study 'the social structure of society (inter-class and intra-class relationships, the social institutions that regulate these relationships), the development and interaction of the systems and organizations within society.'[8]

In more concrete terms, Soviet sociologists have concentrated on the study of occupational strata and ethnic groups. They have also studied attitudes to work and ceremonial life in the broad context of the change towards a more rational and secular social order. These studies use methods of investigation and exposition that are broadly similar to those commonly used by sociologists in other parts of the world.

There are two features of Soviet sociology that call for comment. The first is the pragmatic attitude towards the distinction between Marxist and bourgeois sociology: while it is stressed in principle, it is frequently ignored in practice. The second and much more significant feature is a new way of viewing the relationship between 'base' and 'superstructure'. Soviet sociologists are increasingly arguing that there are various areas of social life that are not covered properly by either, and are best characterized as 'extra-superstructural'; these, according to Afanasyev, include such socio-economic formations as clan, tribe, national group, family and marriage, and some public organizations.[9] Whether this way of representing social reality is a deviation from Marxism or an extension of it, I leave it to the specialists to decide.

The second orientation, which gives to the ideas of Marx a position of importance *within* sociology, has governed the works of

[6] G. Osipov, *Sociology*, Progress Publishers, 1969, p. 9.
[7] Ibid., p. 9.   [8] Ibid., p. 20.
[9] V. G. Afanasyev, *The Scientific Management of Society*, Progress Publishers: 1971, pp. 26–7.

a long line of European scholars from Weber through Mannheim to Aron. While acknowledging the outstanding contribution of Marx to the understanding of social life, these authors have viewed this contribution in a critical light, and, consequently have often been characterized, wrongly in my view, as anti-Marxist. It has been said of Weber that his work was a 'long dialogue with the ghost of Marx', and Mannheim's work has been described as 'bourgeois Marxism'.

The task of sociology, as I see it, is to study the dialectical relationship between ideas and interests, or between the fundamental cultural categories of a society and the distribution of power in it.[10] It is hard to concede that any single historical person (or group of persons owing allegiance to a particular corpus of work) has a superior claim to the appropriation of this task. Among sociologists who wrote in the present century, Weber's work is perhaps the best example of these fundamental concerns. He was concerned not so much with the study of power and of culture in the abstract as with their nature and interrelations in actually existing societies. There are other sociologists whose work shows the same basic concerns, although most have in practice concentrated on one or another aspect of specific human societies.

One can certainly trace back the basic concern with the relationship between ideas and interests to the work of Marx and indeed it is this which provides continuity between Marx and modern sociology. However, it is fruitful to trace continuities only within a living system of ideas. Hence the contribution of Marx to the creation of the sociological perspective acquires meaning only if we regard his theories as not final, his concepts as not fixed and his method as amenable to modification in the light of experience.

From our point of view the first thing to remember is that Marx wrote primarily about particular societies—Germany, France, England—and a particular social transformation. Asian societies in a state of transition a hundred years after Marx's time have their own modes of existence and consciousness. How can we hope to grasp these if, like theologians, we attach ourselves obstinately to the theories, concepts and methods embedded in a given set of texts?

[10] See my 'Ideas and Interests' in André Béteille, *Studies in Agrarian Social Structure*, Oxford University Press. 1973; also André Béteille, 'The Politics of "Non-Antagonistic" Strata', *Contributions to Indian Sociology*, New Series, No. III, 1969.

Finally, we come to the third position according to which Marxism and sociology are by their nature irreconcilable. Perhaps it is the view held by the majority in India among both practising Marxists and academic sociologists, although I am not aware that it has been explicitly formulated by any. It would be interesting to have an Indian expression of this point of view so that we can know whether there are any fresh arguments in its support or whether the arguments are the same as those of European thinkers.

Among Europeans the view that denies the very possibility of a Marxist sociology is expressed most forcefully by Georg Lukács and his followers. Interestingly, in Europe it is the Marxists who reject the possibility of an effective dialogue between Marxism and sociology; the sociologists are more willing to have such a dialogue. In India, on the other hand, both sociologists and Marxists usually view each other with roughly the same degree of suspicion.

Lucien Goldmann, whose work is much respected among European Marxists, wrote in *Le Dieu Caché* that from the viewpoint of Marxism 'sociology is impossible for the Marxist seeks to be practical and revolutionary'.[11] Later, in an article entitled 'Y a-t-il une sociologie marxiste?',[12] he reiterated the same point and argued that a Marxist sociology was not possible. Goldmann's ideas echo those of Lukács who has been probably the most influential Marxist thinker in recent times. Both Lukács and Goldmann would reject any attempt to separate 'judgements of fact' from 'judgements of value' as a denial of revolutionary praxis. For them the core of Marxism lies in this praxis which is based on and is the expression of the fundamental unity of theory and practice. Sociology, they would argue, is by its nature anti-Marxist in so far as it seeks to separate facts from values and defines its task independently of a revolutionary praxis.

The position of Lukács may be stated in yet more concrete terms.[13] All systems of ideas have a class basis. Sociology has its basis in the class interests of the bourgeoisie and is to that extent 'historical'. Marxism is rooted in the class interests of the proletariat and is not 'historical' but 'universal', since in the modern world only the proletariat constitutes the true subject of history. At this point

---

[11] Lucien Goldmann, *Le Dieu Caché*, Gallimard, 1955, p. 98.
[12] Lucien Goldmann, 'Y a-t-il une sociologie marxiste?', *Les Temps modernes* No. 140, October 1957.
[13] Georg Lukács, *History and Class Consciousness*, Merlin Press, 1971.

the Indian sociologist must surely ask who constitute the proletariat or the true subject of history in India. The equation of the organized proletariat with underprivileged humanity, which is implicit in European Marxism, is in the Indian case both false and misleading.

Why is there in India, as elsewhere, this vast seedbed of mutual hostility and suspicion between Marxists and sociologists? I do not for a moment believe that all this can be eliminated by a mere act of will. But an effective dialogue can certainly help to delimit the area of disagreement and to identify its true nature and sources. An effective dialogue will be one which relates itself to the Indian experience and particularly to the agrarian social structure in India.

Mutual hostility is often sustained by a distorted image of the object of one's hostility. It is well known that the founder of Marxism had great contempt for the founder of sociology. Marx wrote in a letter, '. . . as a Party man I have a thoroughly hostile attitude towards Comte's philosophy, while as a scientific man I have a very poor opinion of it.'[14] Now Comte not only invented the term 'sociology', but in Marx's time the subject as such was in Europe identified with his system of positive philosophy. Gurvitch's observation that Marx was the least dogmatic of the founders of sociology becomes clear when we remember that the other principal founder was Comte, for Comte was not only dogmatic, but in his later years an eccentric person. But contemporary sociology—or even the sociology of Durkheim and Weber—bears little resemblance to the somewhat preposterous system constructed by the man who gave their names to both positivism and sociology.

Apart from what one might regard as the accidents of history, there are other issues to consider. It is a matter of experience that the exponents of two systems of idea are often most intolerant of each other not when their ideas are totally different but when they are in most respects basically similar. There is in the realm of ideas as in that of real social relations what the anthropologist describes as 'sibling rivalry'. It is worth considering that the mutual intolerance of Marxists and sociologists owes itself to the basic similarity of their projects rather than to their basic difference.

Both Marxism and sociology concern themselves with the whole of man's experience as a member of society in this world, here and now.

[14] Marx to Beesly in a letter dated 12 June 1871; see Karl Marx and Friedrich Engels, *Correspondence, 1846–1895*, National Book Agency, 1945, p. 277.

Economics and political science deal with specific sectors of society, and history deals with the past rather than the present. The historian can seek refuge in the past, and the economist in his sphere of technical competence. It is difficult to see how the sociologist can avoid confrontation with the Marxist on his own chosen ground.

It is no accident that Marxists can find a place for sociology only by confining the subject within restricted limits. Sartre, for instance, is prepared to accept sociology as an 'auxiliary discipline', but the preference is for a sociology of a very particular kind: 'The more sociology is presented as a hyper-empiricism, the easier is its integration into Marxism.'[15] Similarly, in my experience, Indian Marxists are quite willing to tolerate sociology so long as it confines itself to problems of the 'superstructure'. It hardly needs to be said that sociologist may not feel obliged to accept these arbitrary limitations on their discipline.

Philosophers like Sartre freely castigate sociology for its shallow empiricism, its not having any 'principles', any theory. I think it is only fair to say that sociology has been since its birth in search of a general theory without having really found one. Various theories do emerge from time to time—the general theory of action, symbolic interaction theory, conflict theory—but none of these really corresponds to what would be acceptable as 'theory' in the natural sciences or even in a discipline like economics.

Marx also had a theory about the growth and decay of capitalism in West European society. This theory contained a number of predictions which clearly did not come true. I am prepared to agree with Lukács that one should not be obliged to renounce Marxism solely because some or most of the *results* of Marx's research have been made obsolete by subsequent events or subsequent research.[16] For what really matters is the method or the approach to the study of social reality developed by Marx.

Further, I do not see why one should be obliged to choose between a 'totalizing theory' and a 'shallow empiricism'. This kind of dichotomy is perhaps well suited to the style and temper of a philosopher, but it cannot satisfy those who seek seriously to understand social reality without having either the capacity or the confidence to construct their own general theory. If such a theory is not already available and if it is not within each man's capacity to

[15] Jean-Paul Sartre, *The Problem of Method*, Methuen and Co., 1963, p. 82.
[16] Lukács, *History and Class Consciousness*, op. cit.

construct one, then what is to be done by the ordinary person who might also have a serious interest in understanding human societies?

A sharp dichotomy between 'totalizing theory' and 'shallow empiricism' is not only unreasonable but also pernicious. In those who believe that they have such a theory it encourages an attitude of disdain towards 'mere fact finding'. Many Indian Marxists appear to believe that they already know what are the basic features of this society, what are the mechanisms by which it is being transformed from 'feudalism' to 'capitalism' and what shape it will take in the years to come; they have not found it necessary to study in detail the facts about rural society as their counterparts did in China or Russia. This is the main reason why Marxists have so little to tell us about the *real* characteristics of Indian society as distinct from the characteristics predicated by their theory.

The attitude that we must first have our theory right and then turn our attention to facts is often an attitude of evasion. It is found among both Marxists and academic sociologists. It is an attitude of evasion because either the correct theory is never found or it exists from the very start, in which case the collection of facts is not expected to make much difference.

There is of course much more than an approach to the study of society in the work of Marx, although some believe that this is the most important part of it. It goes without saying that what we are discussing here is Marx's approach to the study of society—his ideas about the structure of societies, their inherent contradictions and the changes which arise from these.

It is not easy to find agreement among the experts on what is the correct Marxist approach to the study of society. There are several texts written by Marx which cannot always be reconciled with each other, and each text can be interpreted in several ways. Perhaps the clearest text is the one in the famous 'Preface' which begins with the statement, 'In the social production of their life, men enter into definite relations that are indispensable and independent of their will . . .' and concludes with the statement: 'The bourgeois relations of production are the last antagonistic form of the social process of production. . . .'[17] This text has the advantage that Marx himself

---

[17] Karl Marx, 'Preface' to *A Contribution to the Critique of Political Economy*, in K. Marx and F. Engels, *Selected Works*, Foreign Languages Publishing House, 1951, Vol. I, pp. 328–9.

described it as representing the approach which he arrived at after long years of study and reflection.

The text referred to contains three sets of statements. There are statements about the structure of society, including its differentiation into basic structure and superstructure. There are statements about contradictions within the base, and between the base and the superstructure; contradictions which manifest themselves in social conflict. And there are statements about change, including a specification of the stages through which societies transform themselves. These statements are tightly linked together in this brief and concise text which is probably more impressive than anything of its kind written by a sociologist before or after.

The very first sentence defines what I would describe as the sociological aims of Marx. One might have difficulties with the exact meaning of the phrase 'social production of their life'. But the statement that 'men enter into definite relations that are indispensable and independent of their will' is not only unambiguous, but one which must be the starting-point of every kind of sociological analysis. Academic sociologists cannot fail to note that it anticipates Durkheim's famous statement that social facts are things and, as things, they are characterized by exteriority and constraint.[18]

The distinction between the base, i.e., the 'totality of relations of production' which constitutes the 'economic structure of society', and the superstructure is also valuable provided one considers it as an heuristic device and not a dogma. It is an error to think that sociologists in general regard all the structures of society to be equally important. What most of them would question is whether the distinction between 'basic structure' and 'superstructure' is one which can be established once and for all; for the rest, many of them assign crucial importance to the economic structure of society.

The contradictions within the base, and between the base and the superstructure are reflected in the conflict of interests among individuals and groups. The idea that interests and their conflicts are socially structured seems to me the most original and fruitful contribution of Marx to sociology. The study of class and of class conflict is rooted in a sociology of interests of which Marx, more than anybody else, laid the foundation. Marx himself saw not only the conflict of classes but the division of labour itself as being rooted in the structure of interests.

[18] Emile Durkheim, *The Rules of Sociological Method*, The Free Press, 1938.

Marx argued that ideals and values which are projected as being general or universal are often masks which cover the interests of a particular class. The mask is not always consciously worn but is for that reason no less there. In *The Eighteenth Brumaire* he showed that not only classes, but organizations such as the bureaucracy might also have 'objective' interests.

The important step in the study of interests is to go beyond the individual and to see how interests are socially structured. 'How is it that personal interests always develop, against the will of individuals, into class interests, into common interests which acquire independent existence in relation to the individual persons, and in their independence assume the form of general interests?'[19] Thus interests have a dual role; they unite people into a class and they divide one class from another although this division may be masked by an ideology.

Marx realized that although interests are socially structured, there is no simple way of identifying their structures; there is in this sense a basic difference of attitude between Marx and the Marxists. Historical materialism might reveal a certain general direction of movement, but the conflict and combination of classes must be related to actually existing interests which are specific to each society at a given stage of its development. *The Eighteenth Brumaire* is a masterly analysis of the complex interplay of interests among the different classes and strata in mid-nineteenth century France.

Indian Marxists have generally assumed a certain structure of interests to prevail in Indian society whereas Marx showed in his writings on France and Germany that such structures are in fact too complex for it to be possible to determine their nature in advance. Academic sociologists have, in their turn, generally ignored the structure of interests in their study of rural Indian society; they have concentrated on common values, and on institutions like caste, kinship and religion which express these common values in their clearest form.

I have stated elsewhere,[20] borrowing an argument from Leach,[21] that social anthropologists who have worked in the Indian field have

---

[19] Karl Marx and Friedrich Engels, *The German Ideology*, Progress Publishers, 1968, p. 270.

[20] Béteille, 'The Politics of "Non-Antagonistic" Strata', op. cit.

[21] E. R. Leach, *The Political Systems of Highland Burma*, G. Bell and Sons, 1954, p. 7.

taken their basic theoretical framework from Durkheim rather than Marx. This has led them to neglect those areas of social life in which the interplay of conflicting interests is most clearly manifest. It is in this context that the themes that have been developed in the earlier essays acquire their significance.

The ownership, control and use of land generate interests that combine and conflict in various ways. The interplay of these interests is easy to observe at the level of interpersonal relations—say, between landlord and tenant, or between cultivator and wage labourer—and such observations are a matter of everyday experience. But what the sociologist owes to Marx is a method, which in India has been used all too sparingly, designed to study these interests in a systematic way, to identify patterns among them and to relate them to the structure of groups and categories, and in particular to the cleavages between classes and between strata.

It should by now be evident why I paid so much attention to the question of what we should mean by a peasant society. The concept of peasant society was introduced into the field of Indian studies through the work of Redfield who was on the whole insensitive to the interplay of conflicting material interests. Those who studied rural India under this kind of inspiration concentrated on the common cultural characterisitics of what they mistakenly categorized as a peasant society, ignoring or neglecting the profound cleavages that have always existed in it.

What is called the peasant community in India is often deeply divided within itself. The Indian village often contains both non-working landowners and landless agricultural workers in addition to other groups and categories. To describe such a village as a community of peasants is to limit the possibility of investigating one of the most interesting features of a social system, i.e., its internal structure of interests. To take as one's point of departure that kind of investigation is to throw open one of the most important features of real societies, their division into conflicting groups and categories.

Just as it is misleading to ignore certain differences, it can also be misleading to ignore certain similarities. By stressing religion and culture, Indian anthropologists have sought persistently to draw a line between tribe and peasantry. I have tried to show that this line is mostly an arbitrary one. Those who work on the land have similar interests whether they speak Bengali or Santali, or practise Hinduism or Animism. There may be differences in their life styles—which are by no means to be discounted—but their life chances are broadly the same.

Finally, the problem of peasants and workers has also to be examined within the framework of a sociology of interests. Are the interests of peasants and of workers fundamentally the same, or are they fundamentally different? Our ideas on these questions are vague and the facts at our disposal are limited and ambiguous. I do not believe that our ideas will ever become clear unless we observe directly the ways in which 'tribesmen', 'peasants' and workers organize their interests in the actual course of their lives.

Marx's analyses of the dynamics of real societies show us that people whose interests appear to be the same are often divided, even as people whose interests appear to be different often come together. It is not easy to follow Marx in this kind of work, for it requires unusual qualities of observation and of imagination. It is much easier and less vexing to apply the 'laws' of dialectical materialism to explain or explain away what is happening or is supposed to be happening in our complex society. But Marx's work is of value to the sociologist not for any laws that he is believed to have discovered but for its profound insight—which is a perennial source of inspiration to students of human society—into the social bases of human conflict.

It was Marx more than any other thinker who made sociologists aware of the inescapable nature of conflict in human societies. And more than anybody else, it was Marx who provided sociology with a method for exposing the mystifications of idea systems which seek to demonstrate the essential harmony of interests in this or that society. Yet Marx also talked about societies free from conflict and antagonism as if he was talking about real societies of the future. And others have used his arguments to assert that some particular historically-existing society has actually progressed beyond the stage of antagonism and conflict.

The famous passage from the 'Preface', referred to earlier, concludes with the statement: 'The bourgeois relations of production are the last antagonistic form of the social process of production—antagonistic not in the sense of individual antagonism, but of one arising from the social condition of life of the individuals; at the same time the productive forces developing in the womb of bourgeois society create the material conditions for the solution of that antagonism. This social formation brings, therefore, the prehistory of human society to a close.'[22] I think it is abundantly clear that Marx meant this statement to be taken literally. I also think that this kind of statement is impossible to reconcile with the sociological perspective, and, if I may add, with the most fruitful and original ideas of Marx himself. What is original in Marx is his understanding of contradiction and conflict: there is nothing original in his conception of a classless society.

The distinction between 'class societies' and 'classless societies' is an important feature of Marxian thought, and from this point of view Marxism differs greatly from modern sociology. Sociologists have studied in detail a far larger range of societies than were accessible to systematic investigation in Marx's time. These studies have shown that inequality and conflict are inherent features of all human societies, including the technologically-primitive tribal societies.

No doubt the distinction made by Marxists can be logically sustained by devising appropriate definitions. As Aron has put it, 'If you define classes with reference to private ownership of the means of production, nothing is easier than to make the former vanish by hoping to suppress the latter.'[23] Since Stalin's time in the Soviet Union and in East European countries scholars have talked about the replacement of 'classes' by 'strata' in their society. The relations between classes are in their view antagonistic, being based on property, while the relations between strata are non-antagonistic, being based on the division of labour.[24]

The contention that the abolition of a particular legal form of the control of the means of production can eliminate antagonism from a society is not an invitation to but an evasion of argument. Since I have made this point elsewhere,[25] I do not wish to dwell on it here. All I would like to say is that there are Marxist texts which are rather well suited to lend authority to this kind of contention.

When Marx wrote about bourgeois society being the last antagonistic form of society and its dissolution as bringing to an end the prehistory of human societies, he had already worked out firm ideas

[22] Marx and Engels, *Selected Works*, op. cit., p. 329.
[23] Raymond Aron, 'Two Definitions of Class' in A. Béteille (ed.), *Social Inequality*, Penguin, 1969, p. 70.
[24] Béteille, 'The Politics of "Non-Antagonistic" Strata', op. cit.
[25] Ibid.

about the kind of social order by which it was to be replaced. The kind of society which would be associated with human history (as opposed to prehistory) is described in vivid detail in *The German Ideology*. In this kind of society 'nobody has one exclusive sphere of activity but each can become accomplished in any branch he wishes; society regulates the general production and thus makes it possible for me to do one thing today and another tomorrow, to hunt in the morning, fish in the afternoon, rear cattle in the evening, criticise after dinner, just as I have a mind, without ever becoming hunter, fisherman, shepherd or critic.'[26] I do not think that even the most ardent Marxist in India would say today that this kind of society exists or is being created in the Soviet Union, although I am not sure that a few of them may not believe this about China.

Whereas Soviet scholars maintain that in their country a society based on classes has been replaced by one based on the division of labour, Marx believed that the dissolution of bourgeois society would lead to the abolition not only of classes but of the division of labour itself. Here we enter perilous ground, for I do not think that this kind of argument can be saved by even the most ingenious definition.

It is clear that for Marx the true source of inequality, exploitation and conflict lay not simply in the system of classes but in the division of labour and, ultimately, in the very fact of labour. Hence it was logical for him to believe that the only way to eliminate conflict, exploitation and inequality was to abolish labour itself. 'The transformation, through the division of labour, of personal powers (relationships) into material powers, cannot be dispelled by dismissing the general idea of it from one's mind, but can only be abolished by the individuals again subjecting these material powers to themselves and abolishing the division of labour.'[27] And further, 'Labour *is* free in all civilized countries; it is not a matter of freeing labour but of abolishing it.'[28]

Now, one can certainly believe that there will be a society in the future where there will be no classes and no division of labour, and where labour itself will cease to exist. But in the cold light of sociological reasoning this kind of belief is no different from the belief in a life after death: it can be neither proved nor disproved.

---

[26] Marx and Engels, *The German Ideology*, op. cit., p. 45.
[27] Ibid., p. 93.   [28] Ibid., p. 224.

It will be a mistake to dismiss the idea of a classless society freed from the division of labour as merely a harmless fantasy. For there are people who believe in it and their belief has important consequences for what they do, what they say and what they write.

Whereas Marx believed that the classless society would come into being in the future, Marxists in our time believe that such a society, or a close approximation to it already exists. Now, sociology as an intellectual discipline must be either fully comparative or nothing, which means that it must view every type of human society with the same critical detachment. This must in the end bring the sociologist into conflict with those who have a jealous attachment to some particular society, whether their own or another.

For thirty years Indian Marxists have had a jealous attachment to the Soviet Union. Soviet society embodied for them the virtues of humanism, justice and scientific progress. In it the worker had at last attained his true worth and dignity, was no longer anyone's inferior, and was free to conduct his life in accordance with principles that were at once humane and scientific. Committed Marxists in India did not doubt the truth of this because they had a theory which predicted the emergence of such a society after the working class Revolution. If they had any doubts they shared them only with others like themselves. To express such doubts in public was to cease to be a committed Marxist, and to become a Trotskyist—or something worse.

Indian Marxists, particularly of the younger generation, have no longer the same attachment to Soviet society. Some of them would go as far as to characterize its system as 'social imperialism'. It is ironic that the attachment to Soviet society should begin to weaken among men of goodwill at precisely that point of time when the Soviet leaders sought to free it from the yoke of Stalinism. All kinds of facts—which the sceptics had always suspected to be there—were brought out after 1956 to show how the old leadership had betrayed the Revolution. Several factors have been responsible for the disenchantment with Soviet society, but the most important of these, at least among younger Marxists in India, is the emergence of a more romantic alternative in China.

Students of human history and human psychology will have to explain how people who have been so rudely disillusioned once can so soon afterwards construct another illusion which is essentially so much like the first. I do not wish to comment on contemporary

Chinese society about which very little is known. But one does not need to know very much about it in order to understand the Marxist attitude to China which is not very different from the earlier attitude towards the Soviet Union about which we do know a few things.

I think it would be no less foolish to cover Soviet or Chinese society with tar and feather than to believe that they embody higher virtues than other human societies have ever attained. The sociologist only demands that all societies—American, British, Chinese, Soviet as well as Indian—be viewed in the same cold, clear light. Marxists have done very well in exposing the inner contradictions of British imperialism, American capitalism and even Indian feudalism, but they have always treated one society—whether Soviet or Chinese—as a privileged exception. Sociology insists on treating all societies alike; it recognizes no privileged exceptions.

7
Marxism, Pluralism and Orthodoxy

> 'If we get a few more of these professors spinning out their theories, we shall be lost.'
> Zinoviev at the Fifth World Congress of the Comintern.

IN THE SECOND half of the twentieth century it is no longer possible to speak of Marxism in the singular: one has to speak of it in the plural. This is true in an obvious sense of Marxist practice, but it is true also of Marxist theory which is my present concern. It will be hard to identify any single approach to the understanding of either man or society—or history, or culture, or nature—that will be accepted as authoritative by all Marxists today. It is said that what is distinctive of the Marxist approach is that it is dialectical. But to describe an approach to society as 'dialectical' is a little like describing it as 'scientific'; Marxists are no more agreed on what they understand by the dialectic than are social scientists on what they understand by science. Marxism has come to signify various things to various people, not only among its adversaries but also among its protagonists. Maxime Rodinson, the renowned Islamic scholar and for many years a member of the French Communist Party, has put it thus: 'For me there is not just *one* Marxism, but *several* Marxisms, all with a common core, it is true, but also with many divergences, each version as legitimate as any other.'[1]

Marxism has grown in depth and variety, not only with the passage of time but also by its diffusion across different parts of the world. Marx's own thought was deeply rooted in the intellectual

[1] Maxime Rodison, *Marxism and the Muslim World*, Orient Longman, 1980, p. 5.

culture of mid-nineteenth century Europe. His concern was primarily with the problems of European society, to the solution of which he applied concepts and categories derived from the resources of European science and European philosophy. In the hundred years since he died, Marx's ideas have found new homes with very different intellectual traditions and requirements. This acclimatization has called for a continuous process of adaptation, innovation and reinterpretation.

The variety of forms taken by Marxism may be seen as a sign of its vitality and its capacity for growth. It is a central part of the Marxist doctrine that life and thought do not remain the same everywhere or for ever, and that changes in the material conditions of life demand changes in the forms of thought. It would be difficult to exaggerate the changes that have taken place in the conditions of life since the time of Marx. Some of them have resulted from ideas implanted by Marx himself and it is not surprising that these changes, by altering the context of his ideas, have given them a new significance.

The divergences in Marxism relate not merely to matters of detail or to points of application, but reach into fundamental questions of theory and method. In other words, not only are there different conceptions of 'mode of production' and 'social formation', or of the relationship between thought and action (or existence and consciousness, or technology and social structure); but these different, or even rival, conceptions are all advocated, forcefully and persuasively, in the name of Marxism.

The interpretation of authoritative texts is an important part of all scholarly disciplines, certainly those concerned with the human sciences. In the absence of some reliance on the authority of texts, intellectual discourse would lose all continuity with the past. Among Marxists intellectual discourse has centred to an unusual degree on the correct interpretation of authoritative texts. Marx occupies a unique position among modern thinkers in the volume and range of interpretations which have taken his ideas as their subject. Marxists, anti-Marxists and ex-Marxists have contended for a hundred years over the true import of his words, and the question of what Marx really meant has been reopened again and again by philosophers, historians, economists, sociologists and others. A well-known contemporary critic has used the phrase 'equivocal and inexhaustible' to characterize his work.[2]

[2] 'Équivoque et inépuisable' is the title used for an essay on Marx by Raymond Aron. See his *Marxismes imaginaires: d'une sainte famille a l'autre*, Gallimard, 1970.

The stupendous volume of interpretative literature has perhaps made the thought of Marx appear more equivocal and inexhaustible than it might by itself be. It has tended to act as a screen between the ordinary reader and what Marx himself wrote, obscuring and confusing even those passages and texts that are simple and easy to read. It is a sign of the greatness of Marx that more people learn his thoughts by what they hear than by what they read, and, even among the highly educated, people can passionately attack and defend these thoughts without being acquainted with them at first hand.

It is not as if the understanding and interpretation of Marx's work present no genuine problems. While these problems should not be exaggerated, they cannot be ignored. Marx was both a scholar trained to the requirements of scholarly discipline and an activist alive to the advantages of quick, not to say instantaneous, response to important political events. He wrote a great deal on a large number of subjects. He also read a great deal and kept himself remarkably well informed on the events of the day. He reacted at once to concrete events and abstract ideas. He adopted more than one style of writing, just as he wrote for more than one kind of audience. In the event, his work does not have the kind of perfect unity which the uninformed too readily assume to be the hallmark of every great mind.

Although Marx wrote a great deal, much of this remained unpublished in his own lifetime. It is doubtful that all of what he left unpublished was intended to be published, although some clearly was. Many of Marx's unpublished writings began to appear in print from 1932 onwards, first in the original and then in various translations. The publication of these manuscripts—in particular the *Economic and Philosophic Manuscripts of 1844* and the *Gründrisse*—became major events in the intellectual history of Marxism. Some felt that they rendered obsolete much of the interpretation of Marx's thought till then considered authoritative. Others maintained that since they were mainly notes, drafts and sketches which Marx chose to leave unpublished, they did not have the same authority as what he himself published in his own lifetime.

Within Marx's varied intellectual output a unique position is occupied by *Capital*. In a sense his entire intellectual life after 1844 centred around the writing of this work, and the study and preparation required for its writing. Only the first of the three volumes of the work we know today as *Capital* was published by Marx in his own life-time and, although he lived for more than fifteen years after its publication, he did not publish any further volumes. Volumes 2 and 3 were put together by Engels, from drafts and notes left behind by Marx, and published after his death. Not surprisingly, Engels was criticized at once—by some for editing the work too little and by others for editing it too much.[3]

The three volumes of *Capital* taken together constitute a monument of intellectual endeavour on a scale rarely attained in history. Nevertheless, the work abounds in gaps, repetitions and obscurities,[4] and one of the greatest economists of the present century was provoked into describing it as 'an obsolete economic textbook'.[5] Whatever may be the final verdict on Marx's theory and method, it is evident that he had rather less certitude about them than many of his followers would like him to have had.[6] Had he arrived at a position which in his own considered judgement appeared as definitive, he would hardly have left his notes and papers in the state in which he did after nearly forty years of concentrated reflection and research. The plain fact is that Marx hesitated between alternative formulations, not merely on points of detail but on fundamental matters, as will be evident from a comparison of the unpublished draft later published as *Gründrisse* and Volume 1 of *Capital*.

Throughout the nineteenth century and until the First War Marxism had its intellectual home in Western Europe, particularly in Germany, France and England.[7] These are the countries in which Marx and Engels lived, and about which they primarily wrote. Although as a body of living ideas Marxism has continued to flourish more actively, more vigorously and more luxuriantly in Western

---

[3] See the 'Supplement' by Engels to Vol. 3 of *Capital*.

[4] Marxist scholars have been from the beginning aware of this, and have tried to provide aids to the reading of *Capital*. See, for instance, the 'Introduction' by Korsch to the 1932 German edition of *Das Kapital*, republished in Karl Korsch, *Three Essays on Marxism*, London: Pluto Press, 1971. A more recent effort is Louis Althusser and Etienne Balibar, *Reading Capital*, NLB, 2nd ed., 1977.

[5] J. M. Keynes, *Essays in Persuasion*, Macmillan, 1933, p. 300.

[6] This is not to suggest that Marx did not on occasion express himself with great self-assurance regarding his discovery of the laws of motion of capitalist society.

[7] One hardly needs to be reminded of the three sources of Marxism—German philosophy, English political economy and French socialism—made famous by Lenin's pamphlet, *The Three Sources and the Three Component Parts of Marxism*, Progress Publishers, 1969.

Europe than elsewhere, the success of the Revolution of 1917 deprived West European Marxism of the unique intellectual authority it had till then enjoyed throughout the world. Ironically, some of the most brilliant Marxists in Western Europe themselves contributed to the devaluation of their own intellectual capital by submitting to the intellectual authority of Soviet Marxism.[8]

The triumph of Soviet Marxism owed a great deal to state power, but it also owed something to the appeal of strong ideas directly and forcefully expressed. Much of what was presented as Marxism in the Soviet Union at the height of Stalin's authority is today derided by the more acute and subtle interpreters of Marxism in the West and their followers elsewhere.[9] For all that, Soviet Marxism had in its day a real intellectual appeal for millions of people whose main, if not sole, exposure to Marxism was through the works of Lenin and Stalin.[10] It will be a mistake to think that that appeal has disappeared forever or can never be quickened to new life again.

The outstanding feature of Soviet Marxism, in contrast with Occidental Marxism, is its unity and continuity as an intellectual system. A great deal of this has been due to the discipline of party and state, but it would be a mistake to ignore what it owes to the Russian intellectual tradition. The kind of materialist doctrine that became established as the official form of Marxism under Stalin in

[8] The fact that Marxism which, in its golden age, represented the highest expression of Western intellectual culture, could establish itself only in what was the most backward part of Europe, had notable consequences for its further development. This point has been tellingly made by Leszek Kolakowski in his monumental *Main Currents of Marxism*, Oxford: Clarendon Press, 1978, 3 vols. See also Isaac Deutscher, *Ironies of History*, Ramparts Press, 1966.

[9] The contrast between Soviet and Western Marxism has now become a commonplace among Marxists themselves. This was not so during Stalin's lifetime. Maurice Merleau-Ponty was perhaps the first notable Marxist to make the contrast between 'Leninism' and what he called 'Occidental Marxism' (see his *Les aventures de la dialectique*, Gallimard, 1955). From the opposite camp, John Plamenatz made the contrast, with characteristic contempt, for the Russian intellect. 'Passing from German to Russian Marxism', he wrote, 'we leave the horses and come to the mules' (John Plamenatz, *German Marxism and Russian Communism*, Longmans, Green & Co., 1954, p. 191).

[10] After the disenchantment with Stalin in the mid-1950s, there was the rise to prominence of Mao Tse-tung, and his celebrated Red Book. I do not discuss Mao's ideas at all as the discussion would take me too far afield to return quickly to my principal argument. But Mao's case would strengthen, not weaken, the argument that there are diverse authoritative versions of Marxism, difficult, if not impossible, to reconcile with each other.

fact enjoyed great influence among Russian Marxists long before the Bolshevik Revolution. Soviet Marxism grew within a particular material and intellectual environment; and, while it is true that the Bolshevik Revolution changed much of the material culture of the old Russia, it is doubtful that it changed as much of the basic categories of its intellectual culture.[11] At any rate, one is struck by the uniformity of the categories used in social analysis from Plekhanov down to the most recent Soviet textbooks of sociology.

Soviet Marxism is characterized by a number of interrelated features. There is, first of all, the adherence to materialism in its various forms: materialist philosophy, dialectical materialism, the materialist interpretation of history. Then there is the pre-occupation with the scientific laws of social dynamics, including the preoccupation with causality and determinism as understood in the natural sciences. Finally, there is the characteristic analytical scheme dividing society into 'base' and 'superstructure', and assigning causal priority to the former over the latter. On all these themes, Soviet Marxism has remained much closer to the spirit of the Second International, with its view of Marxism as the doctrine of 'scientific socialism', than many contemporary forms of Occidental Marxism.[12]

Was Marx himself a materialist? Is it possible to reject materialism—not just 'mechanical' materialism but materialism as such—and still remain a Marxist? Contemporary Western Marxists are by no means in complete agreement on these questions. At any rate, Marx's own writings do not give evidence of the kind of intransigent materialism that has been attributed to him by some of his most authoritative interpreters.

In an essay published shortly after the October Revolution, Bertrand Russell drew attention to the tremendous emphasis on materialism in Bolshevik theory, after pointing to the lack of any necessay connection between 'philosophical materialism' and the 'materialistic conception of history'.[13] The foundations of Russian

[11] I have been struck by the astonishing continuity of Russian culture as reflected in Russian prose literature. The sensibility to which Pasternak and Solzhenitsyn appeal is a Russian sensibility, and basically the same as the one to which Dostoevsky, Tolstoy and Turgenev appealed.

[12] This point was made by Korsch after his break with the Communist Party. See his 'Anti-Critique', first published in 1930 in Karl Korsch, *Marxism and Philosophy*, Monthly Review, 1970.

[13] Bertrand Russell, *The Practice and Theory of Bolshevism*, London: Unwin Books, 1949, pp. 59–60.

Marxism were laid by Plekhanov whose theoretical works remained influential despite his later differences with Lenin. Pre- and post-Revolutionary Russian Marxists, Bolsheviks and Mensheviks, Stalinists and Trotskyists were all influenced by Plekhanov's philosophical writings about which Lenin said that nothing better had been written on Marxism anywhere in the world.

Plekhanov's influential point of view is set out in a work published in 1895 under the title *The Development of the Monist View of History*. It had originally been entitled *In Defence of Materialism*, but that title had to be changed in order to evade censorship. The book sets out to establish the superiority, firstly, of materialism over all other philosophical systems; and, secondly, of dialectical materialism over all other forms of materialism. It is an attack not only on idealism but also on all forms of dualism which refuse to acknowledge the logical and historical priority of matter over mind. The book is written in a didactic style intended to settle once and for all the basic questions of theory and method.

Marxism was represented as materialism of an even more uncompromising kind in a work published fourteen years later by Lenin under the title *Materialism and Empirio-criticism*. The importance of this work for the development of Soviet Marxism can hardly be overstated. In it Lenin pressed the case for partisanship in philosophy and social theory. There were two opposed camps in philosophy—materialism and idealism—between which one had to choose since there was no middle ground. Those who vacillated between the two in the name of 'empirio-criticism', or 'empiriomonism', or plain agnosticism were in fact idealists in disguise who needed to be exposed. In Lenin's words, 'Marx and Engels were partisans in philosophy from start to finish, they were able to detect the deviations from materialism and concessions to idealism and fideism in every one of the 'recent' trends'.[14]

It is now a commonplace among European Marxists that Marx was by no means a partisan for philosophical materialism. Some writers have sought to attribute to Engels the elements of materialism that might have crept into the writings of Marx, inadvertently as it were.[15]

[14] V. I. Lenin, *Materialism and Empirio-criticism*, Progress Publishers, 1977, p. 318.
[15] It has now become a fashion to contrast the shallow materialism (or even positivism) of Engels with the profound dialectics of Marx. See, for instance, Irving Louis Horowitz and Bernadette Hayes, 'For Marx/Against Engels: Dialectics Revisited', *The International Journal of Critical Sociology*, Vol. 1, No. 1, Fall 1975, pp. 21–3. See also Michael Harrington, *The Twilight of Capitalism*, Simon & Schuster, 1976.

These are not new arguments. Lenin was perfectly familiar with them, and his work was in fact directed against those who sought to deny that Marx was a partisan for materialism and to suggest that there might be a basic difference of outlook between Engels and Marx.[16] Differences between Marx and Engels there no doubt were, but it would be strange indeed if Engels had so completely misunderstood Marx on such a fundamental point as some of the anti-materialist adherents of Marxism appear to suggest.[17]

For Plekhanov, Lenin and others, the commitment to materialism meant assigning clear priority to the external order of nature over the internal order of spirit, mind or consciousness. These thinkers saw the social world as an external world, made up of definite relations between men that were indispensable and independent of their will.[18] This external order of society was, in their view, like the external order of nature, governed by immutable laws which could be discovered and formulated, if not with the same exactitude, at least with something of the exactitude of the laws of nature. Marxism provided a method for the discovery and formulation of these laws which far surpassed in range and power the methods of bourgeois political economy and bourgeois sociology.

The case for causality and determinism was made forcefully by Bukharin in a popular manual entitled *Historical Materialism*. 'Society and its evolution are as much subject to natural law as is everything else in the universe', wrote Bukharin[19]; and, again, 'The

---

[16] See Lenin's attack on V. Chernov for his 'attempt to counterpose Marx to Engels' in *Materialism and Empirio-criticism*, pp. 84 ff.

[17] I find the argument for a complete misunderstanding of Marx by Engels or by Kautsky and the other pillars of the Second International to be weak and unconvincing. Marx was not a remote prophet, living in a distant age and out of reach of the people who became his authoritative interpreters after his death. The interpreters to whom the misunderstanding has been attributed lived in the same intellectual environment as Marx and shared the same intellectual presuppositions, and some of them knew him personally and even intimately. If Kautsky—and even Engels—had got Marx all wrong, how can we, at this distance in time and space, ever hope to reconstitute the true Marx?

[18] It is no accident that so many of them—Plekhanov, Lenin, Bukharin—gave such a central place in their interpretation of Marx to the famous statement in the 'Preface' to *A Contribution to the Critique of political Economy* which begins, 'In the social production of their life, men enter into definite relations that are indispensable and independent of their will'.

[19] Nikolai Bukharin, *Historical Materialism: A System of Sociology*, The University of Michigan Press, 1969 (but first published 1921), p. 46.

only correct point of view is that of determinism'[20]. Bukharin's popular manual was attacked by more sophisticated Marxists[21], partly because his formulations were crude and oversimple, but also because Bukharin became an easy target after his estrangement with Stalin. Bukharin's formulations were indeed oversimple; but, then, it was only by virtue of being presented in the form of simple aphorisms that Marxism could take a hold over the minds of millions of ordinary people.

Once again, the idea of a natural science of society, with its presuppositions regarding causality and determinism were more consistently articulated by Engels than by Marx, but it would be disingenuous to pretend that Marx never found the idea appealing or that he ever renounced it clearly and categorically.[22] The idea that Marxism provides the correct scientific explanation of social reality appealed greatly to the best minds of the Second International.[23] It became codified in the Soviet Union and, under the name of *diamat*, it has provided the groundwork for the education of millions of students there and in other socialist countries. It is difficult to see what Marxism would be in the countries of the Third World without the belief in the efficacy of its scientific laws.

According to many Marxists of the present as well as the past, the scientific understanding of society requires giving priority to the laws of economics. As Plekhanov put it, '*The psychology of society is always expedient in relation to its economy, always corresponds to it, is always determined by it*'.[24] The distinction between 'economics' and 'psychology', needless to say, expresses the distinction between

---

[20] Ibid., p. 37.

[21] It received long, hostile reviews from both Lukács and Gramsci. Lukács's review has been republished in *New Left Review*, XXXIX, 1966 as 'Technology and Social Relations' (first published 1925); Gramsci's review is to be found in his *Selections from Prison Notebooks* (see n. 38 below).

[22] The case for a 'natural science of society' is most strongly made by Engels in *Anti-Duhring* to which, it must not be forgotten, Marx had contributed a chapter.

[23] I would include not only Kautsky and adherents of his brand of orthodoxy, but also the Austro-Marxists, a good sample of whose work may be seen in Tom Bottomore and Patrick Goode (eds), *Austro-Marxism*, Oxford: Clarendon Press, 1978. The scholarly contributions of the Austro-Marxists were substantial and, unlike Lukács, Gramsci or Sartre, they took a positive view of empirical sociology; see, for instance, Otto Neurath, *Empiricism and Sociology*, D. Reidel Publishing Co., 1973.

[24] G. Plekhanov, *The Development of the Monist View of History*, Progress Publishers, 1956 (first published 1895), p. 165, italics in original.

base and superstructure (or between social existence and social consciousness), regarded by many, if not most, people as the hallmark of Marxism considered as a scientific doctrine.

Here again, it was Lenin who formulated the distinction most clearly and reacted most sharply to attempts at obliterating it. To put it in his words, 'Social consciousness *reflects* social being—that is Marx's teaching. A reflection may be an approximately true copy of the reflected, but to speak of identity is absurd. Consciousness in general reflects being—that is a general thesis of *all* materialism. It is impossible not to see its direct and *inseparable* connection with the thesis of historical materialism: social consciousness *reflects* social being'.[25] It is possible that Lenin was beguiled by his reading of Engels into misrepresenting Marx. But we still need to explain why so many intelligent interpreters of Marx, many of whom give clear evidence of having read his work, should misrepresent him in exactly the same way.

Marxists have in recent years found it increasingly difficult to apply consistently the distinction between base and superstructure in their analyses of society and history. The recognition of the problem has been followed by various responses. There are those Marxists, like the British historian E. P. Thompson, who would frankly admit that the distinction, once considered useful, no longer appears to be so, and may now be set aside in the interest of a further advance of knowledge.[26] Another kind of response is that of contemporary Soviet sociologists who retain the distinction between 'base' and 'superstructural', but introduce a third category of 'extra-superstructural' factors to accommodate items that do not clearly fall under either base or superstructure.[27]

Not all adherents of Marxism—or, for that matter, all followers of Lenin—have assigned the same fundamental significance to the distinction between base and superstructure. As against such a view, is that which characterizes Marxism in terms of its emphasis on the totality. This was the emphasis of Georg Lukács and those

---

[25] Lenin, *Materialism and Empirio-criticism*, p. 303, italics in original.

[26] E. P. Thompson, *The Poverty of Theory and Other Essays*, Merlin Press, 1978. Thompson has moved away from 'party' or 'orthodox' Marxism to a fairly independent position.

[27] This position goes back to Stalin's famous intervention in the debate over the place of language. It has now become a commonplace of Soviet sociology. See, for instance, V. G. Afanasyev, *The Scientific Management of Society*, Progress Publishers, 1971.

who developed what may be called a hegelian, as opposed to a positivist version, of Marxism.[28] In such a version the relationship between social existence and social consciousness is the relationship between the whole and a part rather than that between two parts, of which one is more important than the other.[29] It would be against the spirit of this approach to contrast 'economics' and 'psychology' with a view to asserting the primacy of the former over the latter.

Soviet Marxists have assigned fundamental importance to method, thereby meaning primarily the scientific method. There is also a great emphasis on method in the work of Lukács—and, likewise, of Sartre[30]—but the term 'method' is here used in a different sense. For Lukács method is, first and foremost, the dialectic, meaning the movement towards unity of subject and object. If it is true that men in society are governed by laws, it is also true that they themselves create these laws, and hence they can understand them best in the very act of their creation. As Marx asks, following Vico, 'And would not such a history be easier to compile, since, as Vico says, human history differs from natural history in this, that we have made the former, but not the latter?'[31]

Lukác's path-breaking work, *History and Class Consciousness*, is not an attempt to subordinate consciousness to material forces. It is, if anything, a celebration of human consciousness as an active agent in the making of human history. As is well known, Lenin, who otherwise praised Bukharin, had remarked that Bukharin did not understand the dialectic. The dialectic as understood by Lukács (or Sartre, or Merleau-Ponty) is, in turn, very different from the sense given to it by Lenin or by Engels.[32] For Lukács there is no such thing as a dialectic of nature: the dialectic has a place only within human history, which is more than merely a continuation of natural history.

[28] The emphasis on 'totality' as against the 'base-superstructure' distinction is characteristic also of the unorthodox and somewhat personal Marxism of Jean-Paul Sartre, *The Critique of Dialectical Reason*, New Left Books, 1976.

[29] Kolakowski sums up the position thus: 'As the whole is always prior to its parts, so the determination of parts by the whole is more fundamental than that of some parts by others' (*Main Currents of Marxism*, Vol. 3, p. 268).

[30] Jean-Paul Sartre, *The Problem of Method*, Methuen & Co., 1963.

[31] Karl Marx, *Capital*, Progress Publishers, 1972, Vol. 1, p. 352, n. 2.

[32] Lukács joined issue with Engels over the latter's concept of the dialectics of nature. See his *History and Class Consciousness*, Merlin Press, 1971 (first published 1923). Especially the Preface to the New Edition (1967), pp. xix ff.

Thus, method for Lukács means, above all, the dialectic whose concern must be with the whole. As he puts it, 'dialectics insists on the concrete unity of the whole';[33] or, again, 'Concrete totality is, therefore, the category that governs reality'.[34] Method in Marxism, according to Lukács (or Sartre) calls for the unity of theory and practice rather than any particular technique of observation or fact finding; the attempt to transform Marxism into scientific sociology is doomed to failure. Marxism, in this view, grows with the growth of the revolutionary consciousness, towards which bourgeois social science takes a negative, if not hostile, stance.

History and Class Consciousness was directed against the Marxism of the Second International in which theory was claiming a life independent of practice. In the very year of its publication, another work, entitled *Marxism and Philosophy* was published by the German Marxist, Karl Korsch, who also took an anti-positivist point of view. Korsch argued strongly against the kind of dualism that sought to drive a wedge between social existence and social consciousness: 'For the *coincidence of consciousness and reality* characterizes every dialectic, including Marx's dialectical materialism'.[35] Korsch's work, like that of Lukács, was denounced by Soviet Marxists. In an 'Anti-Critique', published in 1930, Korsch traced back the roots of the dualism he had earlier attacked to what he considered Lenin's misrepresentation of Marx in *Materialism and Empirio-criticism*.[36]

The preoccupation of Lukács with human consciousness as an active agent in social transformation makes his theory and method very different from theories and methods which rest on ideas of external causality and determinism. Not surprisingly, Lukács was attacked by the theoreticians of the Comintern for propagating 'voluntarism', a charge which Lukács, again not surprisingly, repudiated. Whatever be the merits of these charges and counter-charges, it is difficult when comparing Bukharin and Lukács—who criticized each other—not to be struck by their very different conceptions of the dialectic and of the laws which govern human conduct. The tension between determinism and voluntarism has

---

[33] Ibid., p. 6.   [34] Ibid., p. 10.

[35] Korsch, *Marxism and Philosophy*, pp. 77–8.

[36] Ibid., pp. 89–126. It may be noted that *Materialism and Empirio-criticism* appeared in a German translation only in 1927, and was probably not accessible to either Lukács or Korsch in 1923.

become even more marked in the discussion of Marxism that has grown in Western Europe since the mid-1950s.

Among Marxists who have attacked determinism and asserted the primacy of the human will, none has enjoyed greater respect, at least since the time of Lenin, than Gramsci. Gramsci owes his unique place in contemporary Marxism as much to his highly original presentation of it as to the conditions under which he lived and wrote.[37] Like Lukács, Gramsci also wrote a long critique of Bukharin's *Historical Materialism*, and this critique is important because it brings out the difference between his approach and the approach not only of Bukharin but of what became established as Soviet Marxism.

In the course of his critique of Bukharin, Gramsci wrote,

> It is well known, moreover, that the originator of the philosophy of praxis [Marx] never called his own conception materialist and that when writing about French materialism he criticizes it and affirms that the critique ought to be more exhaustive. Thus he never uses the formula 'materialist dialectic', but calls it 'rational' as opposed to 'mystical', which gives the term 'rational' a quite precise meaning.[38]

Whether true or false, this view of Marxism is strikingly, if not startlingly, different from the textbook representation of it as being first and foremost a form of materialism.[39] Needless to say, it has implications for a critique not only of Bukharin's *Historical Materialism* but also Lenin's *Materialism and Empirio-criticism*.[40]

[37] Kolakowski has written, 'It was undoubtedly thanks to his imprisonment that Gramsci was able to remain a member of the Communist party' (*Main Currents of Marxism*, Vol. 3, p. 226).

[38] Antonio Gramsci, *Selections from Prison Notebooks*, Lawrence & Wishart, 1971, pp. 456-7.

[39] It is now becoming increasingly apparent even to Marxists and Marxist sympathisers that there is a tension, perhaps an inherent tension, between materialism and dialectic. See Merleau-Ponty, *Les aventures de la dialectique*. For Lenin, of course, there was no problem in combining dialectic with materialism; Marx and Engels had emphasized the *dialectical* side of dialectical materialism, but one might just as well emphasize its *materialist* side. See Lenin, *Materialism and Empirio-criticism*, p. 309 ff.

[40] Gramsci castigates Plekhanov, 'who, in reality, despite his assertion to the contrary, relapses into vulgar materialism' (*Selections From Prison Notebooks*, p. 387), but does not, so far as I am aware, take issue with Lenin on his materialism.

If we follow Gramsci, materialism is a metaphysic which obstructs historical understanding, which is the only form of understanding appropriate to a subject concerned with human beings. Gramsci's approach to Marxism is a historicist approach, consciously opposed to every form of positivism. The subject matter of history being radically different from that of the natural sciences, their methods must also be different.

Gramsci's historicism has appealed to many Marxists in the West, but by no means to all. A highly influential version of Marxism emerged in the sixties of the twentieth century under the leadership of the French structuralist, Louis Althusser. As against a humanistic and historicist interpretation, Althusser's structuralist interpretation of Marx sought to put back the emphasis on 'laws', 'determinants' and 'structures', on the basis of a sharp distinction between the earlier and the later work of Marx. In this version, the later, more mature and scientific work of Marx as exemplified in *Capital* should be seen as superseding his earlier work which, up to the period of *The German Ideology*, was permeated by 'humanistic' and 'historicist' categories.[41]

It will be clear from what has been said above that Marxism, as theory and method, has retained much greater unity and continuity in the Soviet Union than outside it. In Western Europe several different versions of Marxism have succeeded each other, particularly in the last twenty-five years, and differences arising from national intellectual traditions, as between German and French Marxism or between French and English Marxism, are also discernible.[42] The co-existence of these various interpretations of Marxism—in some ways complementary and in other ways difficult to reconcile—enables Marxism to retain and perhaps extend its appeal among all those who have a real interest in the understanding of society and history.

The plurality of approaches within Marxism must be seen in the light of what has been and continues to be another important, if not

---

[41] See Louis Althusser, *For Marx*, Harmondsworth: Penguin Books, 1969. For a trenchant critique, see Leszek Kolakowski, 'Althusser's Marx', *The Socialist Register*, 1971, pp. 111–28. See also Raymond Aron, 'Althusser ou la lecture pseudo-structuraliste de Marx' in *Marxismes imaginaires*, pp. 193–354.

[42] For an account of French Marxism in its social and intellectual setting, see George Lichtheim, *Marxism in Modern France*, Columbia University Press, 1966; for a lively contrast between French and English Marxism, see E. P. Thompson, 'The Peculiarities of the English' in *The Poverty of Theory and Other Essays*.

intrinsic, feature of it, namely, the preoccupation of Marxists with orthodoxy. By this I simply mean that Marxists are concerned not only with the correct understanding of the world but, over and above that, and to an unusual degree, with the correct interpretation of a particular body of writings. Thus, debates among Marxists, and between Marxists and their adversaries, move along two intersecting scales: on the one hand whether, for instance, base in fact determines superstructure or psychology merely reflects economics; on the other, what Marx really meant by the various observations he made on such subjects.

Orthodoxy, as orthodox Marxists are ready to point out, is not the same thing as dogmatism. Dogmatism indicates unwillingness to reconsider one's initial position in the light of new facts or facts not considered earlier. Marxism would not have survived as an intellectual system had it refused to respond to the momentous changes taking place in the real world. The recognition of changes that call for the replacement of old ideas by new has been a conspicuous feature of European Marxism. And as one eloquent advocate of orthodoxy has argued, one may renounce many, even most of the substantive propositions formulated by Marx without ceasing to be an orthodox Marxist.[43]

The idea of orthodoxy, which has its widest use in the domain of religion, is difficult to define in the context of Marxism, which is secular and scientific in its orientation. Not all Marxists make a case for orthodoxy, explicitly and systematically, but the striking thing is that so many do. The orthodoxy of Kautsky, once widely acknowledged, was later repudiated by Lenin. Lukács sought to give a new meaning to the idea of orthodoxy so as to harmonize it with Lenin's practice, but his formulation was condemned by Lenin's heirs in Moscow.

Not only are various forms of orthodoxy opposed to each other, but orthodoxy as such is opposed to revisionism. The term 'revisionist' is difficult to define since it may be used in a loose sense by the advocates of one kind of orthodoxy to denounce or revile the

---

[43] Georg Lukács, 'What is Orthodox Marxism?' in *History and Class Consciousness*. But as against this, one may reasonably ask, as Bottomore has done, 'More generally, what is the sense of saying that Marxist orthodoxy consists in accepting Marx's method, if at the same time it should be the case that this method produces nothing but false propositions'? (T. B. Bottomore, *Sociology as Social Criticism*, Pantheon Books, 1974, p. 105.)

advocates of another. But revisionists in the strict sense make no pretence at orthodoxy. They are those who call for a serious re-examination of the tenets of Marxism, including some of its fundamental tenets, while seeking to remain within the Marxist tradition.

The attack on the revisionism of Bernstein by Kautsky and the custodians of orthodoxy brought to light a fundamental contradiction in the Marxism of the Second International. For Marxism, as it was presented by the theoreticians of the Second International, was a positive science: it was the scientific aspect of Marxism that they most strongly recommended. Why should it be inherently wrong, as the orthodox seemed to say it was, to revise a body of knowledge that claimed to be a positive science? Marxist ideas of orthodoxy and revisionism are difficult to accommodate within the domain of positive science which regards the capacity for revision as a virtue and the claim of orthodoxy a defect.

The superior merit of Lukács over Kautsky lay in this, that he did not seek to combine the claim of orthodoxy with the claim that Marxism was a positive science. For Lukács (as also for Korsch and Gramsci), Marxism was not a positive science, not even a superior form of it, but stood in opposition to it. Orthodoxy in Marxism involved not a defence of but an attack on empiricism which, according to Lukács, constituted the foundation of bourgeois social science. The obsession with facts as they are is a feature of the 'Contemplative' as opposed to the 'dialectical' method which is the defining feature of Marxism.[44] Any attempt to revise Marxism in the name of facts as they are given 'must lead to over-simplification, triviality and eclecticism'.[45]

Lukács was the first to articulate in a systematic way a new view of orthodoxy in Marxism, centering not on scientific socialism but on revolutionary praxis. In 'What is Orthodox Marxism?' and in the other essays published together as *History and Class Consciousness*, he presented his case with unsurpassed verve and sophistication. Lukács's view of Marxism as revolutionary praxis rather than scientific socialism found its echo in the writings of a number of his contemporaries, notably Korsch and Gramsci.

[44] This is how Lukács confronted the argument that facts seemed to go against the Marxist doctrine: 'If, in Hegel's terms, becoming now appears as the truth of Being, and process as the truth about things, then this means that the *developing tendencies of history constitute a higher reality than the empirical "facts"* '. (*History and Class Consciousness*, p. 181, italics in original).

[45] Ibid., p.1.

The shift in orientation from scientific socialism to the philosophy of praxis was precipitated by the momentous events of the Bolshevik revolution. Gramsci hailed these events in a newspaper article entitled 'The Revolution Against *Das Kapital*'. Korsch called for a closer union between revolutionary theory and practice, and Lukács presented his new vision of orthodox Marxism. All three were calling for a fuller appreciation from occidental Marxists of the significance, not merely the *practical* significance but also the *theoretical* significance, of the revolution made by Lenin and his associates.

History and Class Consciousness by Lukács and *Marxism and Philosophy* by Korsch were both published in 1923. It seems to me that these two works (and the work of Gramsci) provide a far more powerful philosophical support for Lenin's practice than does Lenin's own philosophical treatise, *Materialism and Empirio-criticism*, published between the abortive revolution of 1905 and the successful one of 1917.[46] But Lenin's heirs in Moscow, those who had helped him make the October Revolution and were still fighting bitterly to save it, thought otherwise. At the historic Fifth World Congress of the Comintern in 1924, Zinoviev led the attack on Korsch and Lukács, denouncing their work as 'theoretical revisionism'.[47]

The question still remains as to why the Soviet leadership reacted so sharply against the attempt to establish a new orthodoxy that would vindicate the revolution that was its own creation. Part of the answer lies in what may be described as the inertia of intellectual categories. The intellectual categories of Lenin's heirs were those established as authoritative by Plekhanov, in which matter was prior to mind, and psychology expedient to economy; and the plain

---

[46] This is not to say that Lenin hesitated to strike when the opportune moment came or that he did not produce arguments in support of such action. It must not be forgotten that Lenin spelled out the active role of the vanguard party in *What is to be Done?* before he wrote *Materialism and Empirio-criticism*. My point is a more limited one, namely, that there is a yawning gap between Lenin's political activism and his theory of knowledge, the presuppositions and implications of his materialist philosophy which in fact became the established doctrine of the Soviet schools. This point has been noted by others before. Lichtheim, for instance, wrote, 'Though Lenin's *practice* was voluntaristic, his philosophy implied a belief in immutable laws impervious to human volition' (*Marxism in Modern France*, p. 95, n. 25, italics in original). The only thing that I would like to add is that Lenin's philosophy did not merely *imply* this, but hammered the point with singular tenacity.

[47] Fifth Congress of the Communist International: Abridged Report, published by the Communist Party of Great Britain, p. 17.

fact is that those who bring about a revolution in the real world do not necessarily bring one about in their own categories of thought. Without a fundamental change in those categories, the new proposals for orthodoxy were bound to appear 'idealistic' and 'voluntaristic', and to be rejected as such.

Lukács, Korsch and other 'idealist deviationists' were not merely celebrating the Bolshevik revolution; they were presenting their arguments in a particular idiom that had its roots in Hegel's philosophy. Russian Marxism had absorbed very little of this idiom, which might indeed have appeared as an encumbrance to those who saw the main intellectual task after the Revolution to be that of codification. If, as Lukács and Korsch were arguing, Marxism was the intellectual expression of the revolutionary movement of the proletariat, it had to be brought within the intellectual reach of the working class. Soviet Marxists might, with some justice, say that it was they, and not professors like Lukács and Korsch, who were in reality carrying Marxism to the workers.

Codification might make Marxism easy for the workers, but it generates its own orthodoxy. The speed with which Soviet Marxism under Stalin displaced all other claimants to orthodoxy might have something to do with its intellectual form and content, but cannot be explained solely by that. Questions of orthodoxy never are fully resolved on the merits of ideas; they are settled in the end by the struggle for power.

Marxism is unique among modern intellectual systems not only in its insistence on orthodoxy, but in its attempt to create theoretical grounds for giving the party a determining voice on questions of orthodoxy. It is not enough to point to the part played by the Stalinist leadership in imposing a particular kind of orthodoxy through the use or threat of force; one must recognize also the legitimacy accorded to the party in the writings of Lukács, Gramsci and others in deciding on questions of orthodoxy. Even if it is true that Stalin did not endorse the theories of Lukács, or Gramsci the practices of Stalin, the two developments were taking place simultaneously in what appeared from the outside as broadly the same movement.

It is not unusual to view Marx as a social scientist, and to compare his intellectual system with the intellectual systems of other social scientists, e.g., Max Weber or Keynes. But neither of the latter generated orthodoxies at all comparable to those established in the name of Marx. In purely intellectual terms, the only possible comparison might be with the system created by Freud. But it was never a part of any Freudian orthodoxy to use a political party as the vehicle of its true expression. The practical and theoretical significance of the party in Marxism gives to Marxist orthodoxy a totally different character from all contemporary social science systems.

Those, like Gramsci and Lukács, who, after the Bolshevik revolution, sought to free Marxist theory from the straitjacket of determinism imposed on it by the orthodoxy of the Second International, sought at the same time to give a central role to the party in the articulation of working-class consciousness. The party had some authority in deciding on questions of theory throughout the period of the Second International. But it was only after the Bolshevik revolution that the essence of Marxism was linked to the revolutionary party with the aid of the most complex and ingenious theoretical reasoning.

Lukács and Korsch attacked the orthodoxy of the Second International for representing Marxism as a positive science whose truth was independent of any political movement. In their view Marxism could have a valid existence only as 'the theoretical expression of the revolutionary movement of the proletariat';[48] and never independently of it. For Lukács, as we have seen, method is all-important, but method consists not of a set of procedures for collecting and analysing facts, but, above all, in adopting what he calls 'the stand-point of the proletariat'. It is this standpoint rather than any detached intellectual skill that is the guarantee of true insight. As Lukács puts it, 'the knowledge yielded by the standpoint of the proletariat stands on a higher scientific plane objectively';[49] for only the proletariat is destined to become the 'identical subject-object of history'.[50]

But what is the stand-point of the proletariat? And what is the class consciousness of the proletariat? Lukács is keen to point out that he is talking not about 'empirical' or 'psychological' consciousness, but about 'real' or 'historical' or 'imputed' consciousness:

> Now class consciousness consists in fact of the appropriate and rational reactions 'imputed' [*zugerechnet*] to a particular typical

[48] The phrase is from Korsch, *Marxism and Philosophy*, p. 42.
[49] Lukács, *History and Class Consciousness*, p. 163.
[50] Ibid., p. 197.

position in the process of production. This consciousness is, therefore, neither the sum nor the average of what is thought or felt by the single individuals who make up the class.[51]

And it is here that the role of the party becomes decisive, for 'the Party is the historical embodiment and the active incarnation of class consciousness';[52] and, again, 'the Party is assigned the sublime role of *bearer of the class consciousness of the proletariat and the conscience of its historical vocation*'.[53]

Gramsci has been hailed as the exponent of a humanist form of Marxism, but it is to Gramsci that we owe the most persuasive theoretical attempt at an apotheosis of the political party. *The Modern Prince* is one of the great works of social and political theory, and it is entirely free from the pyrotechnic characteristic of Lukács's writing. Gramsci played a leading part in founding the Italian Communist Party, and his work derives its strength and appeal from its sincerity as much as its originality. When Gramsci spoke of working-class consciousness he did not mean an imputed consciousness accessible to only a select few; the actual or empirical worker and his view of the world never ceased to engage his attention.

We have to remember that in Gramsci's perspective the purely organizational side of the party was subordinate to its cultural and intellectual life. The party was to be not merely an instrument for the capture of power; it was to be above all a school for the creation of a new culture, a new outlook and a new way of life. Men could not leave it to history to change things in accordance with some preordained law of progress. The initiative lay with them to create a new life for themselves in the pursuit of their own collective needs and aspirations.

Gramsci had a genuine belief in the efficacy of the human will and of human ideas, and sought to give these a central place in his conception of Marxism. There could be no revolution in real life without a revolution in ideas, and the revolution in ideas would not

---

[51] Ibid., p. 51. Those with even a superficial acquaintance of the literature cannot fail to note in this an echo of Marx who wrote in *The Holy Family*, 'It is not a question of what this or that proletarian, or even the whole proletariat, at the moment *regards* as its aim. It is a question of *what the proletariat is*, and what, in accordance with this *being*, it will historically be compelled to do'. (K. Marx and F. Engels, *The Holy Family*, Progress Publishers, 1975, p. 44, italics in original.)

[52] Lukács, *History and Class Consciousness*, p. 42.

[53] Ibid., p. 41, capitals and italics in original.

come about as a mere byproduct or after-effect of the revolution in material conditions. In all this the intellectual function was of crucial importance, but it could not be performed from above or outside; it had to become a constitutive part of the working-class movement.

Gramsci thought of a new kind of intellectual, organically linked with the working-class movement, and a new framework for his intellectual activity, namely, the political party. He wrote, 'That all members of a political party should be regarded as intellectuals is an affirmation that can easily lend itself to mockery and caricature. But if one thinks about it, nothing could be more exact'.[54] In Gramsci's view it was the party alone that could weld together the older 'traditional' intellectuals with the new intellectuals whose growth was organically linked with the growth of the working class.

Without active intellectual engagement the party would degenerate into a lifeless machine. But if intellectual activity was necessary to the health and well-being of the party, the party was no less indispensable to the kind of intellectual life Gramsci considered appropriate to Marxism. One cannot emphasize too strongly the central place assigned to the party in Gramsci's philosophy of praxis. The party *is* the 'modern Prince', the protagonist of revolutionary praxis in the modern world, and as such it has a historical mission of the highest importance: 'In men's consciences, the Prince takes the place of the divinity or the categorical imperative, and becomes the basis for a modern laicism and for a complete laicization of all aspects of life and of all customary relationships'.[55] It would be a grave error to think that the supreme role assigned to the political party in the direction of intellectual life can be detached from Gramsci's 'philosophy of praxis' without changing its character altogether.

These considerations leave us with a number of questions concerning contemporary debate, on which I would like to raise only one in conclusion. The question with which I would like to conclude concerns the prospect of an independent Marxism in India today. I raise this question because I believe that the involvement of the party in Marxist thought, or even its control of it, in the Stalin years was not a mere aberration of Stalinist practice but a logical corollary

[54] Gramsci, *Selections From Prison Notebooks*, p. 16.
[55] Ibid., p. 133.

of Marxist theory in at least some authoritative versions of it. The practice has changed, no doubt, but the implications for theory of this change in practice are not always candidly discussed.

Orthodoxy on questions of theory under the direction of a political party cannot mean the same thing today as it did during Stalin's time. The simple fact is that there is no longer any political party that can speak with the same authority to all Marxists that Communist parties all over the world, including India, did only a generation ago. There are divisions between national Communist parties even as there are divisions within the international Communist movement. Hardly any Communist party has today the moral authority to claim a determining role in settling questions of theory. Stalin's *Short Course* was intended to settle questions not only of practice but also of theory; it is hard to visualize another such work acquiring the same kind of authority in the 1980s.

It is necessary to discuss the tension that has existed and continues to exist between what may be called 'academic Marxism' and 'party Marxism', and to examine its sources. There *is* an academic Marxism, distinct from party Marxism—and increasingly so—no matter how much its proponents might defer to the intellectual authority of Lukács or Gramsci. Their relationship must be examined, not merely in a general and abstract way, but in the context of each national tradition with its particular intellectual culture and its particular political compulsions. It is often said that the social sciences have had very little autonomous growth in India, that their growth has followed paths laid down in Europe and America; there is truth in this, but the truth applies as much to Indian Marxism as to Indian social science.

If we look at the record since 1956, the intellectual contributions of independent Marxists will appear substantial, at least in Western Europe. One thinks of Habermas in Germany, or Rodinson in France or E. P. Thompson in England. My own view is that the independent Marxist, mainly in the academic world but also outside, will extend his intellectual influence in the years to come, and in doing so will look over his shoulders less and less to see how the party reacts. Until now, at least in India, he has stood on somewhat uncomfortable ground, between the liberal academics who see intellectual freedom as an end in itself and the orthodox Marxist who sees the authority of the party as supreme. The academic Marxist has perhaps less reason than he thinks to be on the defensive in his orientation towards the party. Marxist theory, since at least the time of Lenin, has combined the critique of bourgeois society with the exaltation of the Communist party. It has sought to make partisanship the basis of every kind of commitment. The spirit of Marxism requires that the critique of capitalist society be extended to other forms of society as well. Such a critique must have a basis in some kind of social commitment, but it is now too late to argue that that commitment can be guaranteed only by a political party.

8
Is there a Marxist Anthropology?

IS THERE A Marxist anthropology? It may appear capricious to ask this question at a time of unprecedented enthusiasm for Marxism among social anthropologists in Britain, France and America. Yet the question has been asked for more than fifty years in relation to the cognate discipline of sociology, and the answers given to it there have been by no means clear or unequivocal.[1]

Any discussion of the scope or possibility of a Marxist anthropology must begin by recognizing the plurality of conceptions people have of both anthropology and Marxism. I would like to disclaim any pretence at dealing even-handedly with all the available conceptions, or even the most important among them, of either Marxism or anthropology.[2] My attempt will be to confront a particular conception of the one with a particular conception of the other. I hope that my choice will not appear altogether arbitrary in either case, although such a choice is bound by its nature to be personal. It should be said at the outset that I make no claim to being a Marxist and that my credentials as an anthropologist are easily open to question.

The two conceptions that I would like to bring face to face are of anthropology as 'the study of other cultures' and of Marxism as 'the philosophy of praxis'. I would like to argue that these are both valid

---

[1] For a provocative response, going back to the fifties, see Lucien Goldmann, 'Y a-t-il une sociologie marxiste?', *Les temps modernes*, No. 140, October 1957, pp. 729–51.

[2] I exclude from consideration anthropology in the special sense of 'philosophical anthropology' as developed within the German intellectual tradition. For a consideration of the place of Marxism in anthropology in this sense, see George Markus, *Marxism and Anthropology*, Van Gorcum, 1978.

and authentic conceptions, the first of anthropology and the second of Marxism. What exactly are the problems in establishing and maintaining a working relationship between the study of other cultures and the philosophy of praxis? This seems to me to be the fundamental question to be asked in a discussion of Marxist anthropology, and I am struck by the facility with which it is evaded by anthropologists who are keen to see their discipline enriched by its association with Marxism.[3]

The problem on which I am trying to focus attention will vanish to a large extent if we represent Marxism as a positive science and social anthropology as the comparative study of human societies in general. Indeed, it may be argued that the aim of social anthropology as defined by some of its ablest exponents has been to establish nothing less than a fully comparative sociology. On the other side there have been Marxists who have claimed with considerable authority that their theoretical objective has been to establish an empirical science of society on a level with the natural sciences. Why should there be any problem in bringing together two approaches to the study of society that are both empirical, general and scientific?

Very little will be gained by making the problem of the relationship between Marxism and anthropology vanish by a choice of convenient definitions. It is a fact of recent intellectual history—in the West as well as outside—that Marxism and sociology have been at odds with each other to such an extent that a British sociologist, well known for his sympathy with Marxism, has said that we should perhaps speak not so much of a Marxist sociology as of a 'Marxist anti-sociology'.[4] The tensions between Marxism and anthropology lie even deeper and are perhaps for that reason less readily visible. The advantages in creating a closer relationship between anthropology and Marxism may be both real and obvious, but the difficulties in maintaining such a relationship are no less real, although they may not be equally obvious.

Anthropology as the Study of Other Cultures

What do we mean when we describe anthropology as the study of other cultures? It is important to distinguish between the aims,

[3] It is on the whole evaded by Maurice Bloch in his otherwise excellent recent book, *Marxism and Anthropology. The History of a Relationship*, Clarendon Press, 1983.

[4] T.B. Bottomore, 'Marxist Sociology' in *International Encyclopedia of the Social Sciences* (David L. Sills, ed.), New York: Macmillan and Free Press, 1968, Vol. 10, p. 52. See also his *Marxist Sociology*, London: Macmillan, 1975, especially chapter 3, 'Marxism against Sociology'.

including the scope and method, of anthropology and the work actually done by anthropologists. Both have changed over time and there has always been some disparity between the two. Anthropologists have of course been aware of this disparity but they have not all responded to it in the same way. On the whole, anthropologists have been less concerned with what anthropology is than Marxists have been with what Marxism is, the question of orthodoxy being very differently considered in the two cases. It is well-known that disagreement on even fundamental questions of scope and method has not prevented anthropologists from working in close association with each other.[5]

In order to avoid going too far back into history I would like to begin with a consideration of the conception of anthropology characteristic of the work of Radcliffe-Brown. There are several advantages in doing this. Firstly, Radcliffe-Brown occupied a commanding position among anthropologists in his own country and throughout the Commonwealth at a time not very remote from our own. Secondly, he was tireless in his effort to define the scope and method of anthropology, expressing himself with great force and clarity on the subject.[6] And thirdly, Radcliffe-Brown came close to establishing a conception of anthropology which is in some ways the opposite of the one which I wish here to explore.[7]

As is well known, Radcliffe-Brown sought to develop anthropology into a natural science of society. He was a tireless advocate of the comparative method, and he argued that a natural science of society which was truly general and comparative could be created only by applying the same rules of procedure to the study of all human societies from the simplest to the most complex. Such an

---

[5] An example that immediately comes to mind is the long and I believe cordial relationship between Radcliffe-Brown who sought to make anthropology into a natural science and Evans-Pritchard who viewed it as a branch of humanistic studies.

[6] See A.R. Radcliffe-Brown, *A Natural Science of Society*, Glencoe: Free Press, 1957; also his *Method in Social Anthropology* (ed. M.N. Srinivas), Chicago: University of Chicago Press, 1958. Radcliffe-Brown was also a very persuasive speaker as has been attested by a somewhat unsympathetic witness, E.R. Leach in his Radcliffe-Brown Lecture: 'Radcliffe-Brown's academic influence depended much more on what he said than on what he wrote. He had a large, imposing physical presence, he was very fluent, and he was superficially knowledgeable about a great variety of subjects' (Edmund Leach, 'Social Anthropology: A Natural Science of Society?' *Proceedings of the British Academy*, Vol. 62, 1976, p. 8).

[7] This conception is most clearly set forward in Radcliffe-Brown, *A Natural Science of Society*.

approach cannot accommodate a radical separation between either primitive and advanced societies or other societies and one's own society. It is not surprising that for Radcliffe-Brown social anthropology and comparative sociology were one and the same thing, not in practice perhaps but certainly in principle.

It is forgotten how great Radcliffe-Brown's influence on anthropology was in Britain at a time when the subject was rapidly expanding there. His influence extended outside Britain as well. An anthropology freed from the taint of its historical association with 'primitive', 'savage' or 'uncivilized' societies has an immediate appeal in countries outside Europe and America. Indeed, it is difficult to see what students of society in Africa and Asia are to do with an anthropology which is tied to the study of 'primitive' societies. In India a social anthropologist would rather call himself a sociologist and I believe that this is even more the case in Africa.

One cannot see how anthropology can establish itself as a general, comparative science of society without merging with sociology or displacing it. Radcliffe-Brown's claims on behalf of anthropology acquired some force in Britain precisely because sociology had not found a place for itself there. With the rapid expansion of sociology in Britain after his death, those claims began to lose much of their force.

In any case, the claims Radcliffe-Brown made in theory on behalf of social anthropology were never pursued very far in practice. Radcliffe-Brown's own specialised work was on the Australian Aborigines and the Andaman Islanders, types of society chosen for their simplicity, if not their remoteness from modern civilization.[8] The two collections of studies, one on political systems and the other on kinship and marriage, which became landmarks in British social anthropology and which both drew their inspiration from Radcliffe-Brown, were devoted to tribal or at least small-scale societies.[9] The title chosen for the collection of Radcliffe-Brown's

---

[8] Radcliffe-Brown's work on the Australian Aborigines was published in several papers, notably, 'Three Tribes of Western Australia', *Journal of the Royal Anthropological Institute*, Vol. 43, 1913, pp. 143–94; and 'The Social Organization of Australian Tribes', *Oceania*, Vol. 1, pp. 34–63, 206–46, 322–41, 426–56, 1930–1. His work on the Andaman Islanders was published in a monograph, *The Andaman Islanders*, Cambridge University Press, 1922.

[9] M. Fortes and E. E. Evans-Pritchard (eds.), *African Political Systems*, London: Oxford University Press, 1940 (with a Preface by A. R. Radcliffe-Brown); and A. R. Radcliffe-Brown and C. Daryll Forde (eds.), *African Systems of Kinship and Marriage*, Oxford University Press, 1950.

own papers published towards the close of his life was *Structure and Function in Primitive Society*.[10]

Although Radcliffe-Brown made far-reaching claims for social anthropology as the theoretical natural science of society, he was always aware that it was in fact concerned mainly with the study of primitive or pre-literate societies. On the one hand he saw that, if there was to be a general and comparative science of human societies, there could be only one such science and not two, one for primitive and the other for civilized societies.[11] On the other hand, the division of labour between students of the two kinds of society was too well established in Europe and America to be ignored or wished out of existence. In a textbook on which he began work after retirement from Oxford, he wrote, 'Social anthropology may be defined as the investigation of the nature of human society by the systematic comparison of societies of diverse types, with particular reference to the simpler forms of society of primitive, savage or non-literate peoples'.[12]

It is no accident that Radcliffe-Brown sought to establish his natural science of society by promoting the idea of social structure—or social morphology[13]—at the expense of culture. 'Culture' for him represented 'content', what was particular, whereas his interest was in the general. 'You cannot have a science of culture', he wrote. 'You can study culture only as a characteristic of a social system. Therefore, if you are going to have a science, it must be a science of social systems.'[14] He declared that it would be good if the concept of culture could be banished from anthropological discourse.

But culture, which to Radcliffe-Brown appeared an embarassment, is in a very important sense what anthropological study is actually about. At the height of Radcliffe-Brown's influence in Britain the belief was created that the study of culture was both unscientific and un-British, that it was a characteristic of the

---

[10] A. R. Radcliffe-Brown, *Structure and Function in Primitive Society*, Cohen and West, 1952.

[11] Radcliffe-Brown, *Method in Social Anthropology*, p. 39.

[12] Ibid., p. 111.

[13] In this Radcliffe-Brown was a follower of Durkheim. See E. Durkheim, *The Rules of Sociological Method*, Free Press, 1966, especially chapter 4, 'Rules for the Classification of Social Types'.

[14] Radcliffe-Brown, *A Natural Science of Society*, p. 106.

American approach to anthropology.[15] Even in Radcliffe-Brown's lifetime this belief had very little basis. Malinowski, who was Radcliffe-Brown's principal adversary in Britain, contributed as much as any other anthropologist to the understanding of culture; and Evans-Pritchard, who was Radcliffe-Brown's successor at Oxford, devoted himself primarily to the humanistic understanding of the ideas, beliefs and values of people lacking the resources of literacy.[16]

It is Evans-Pritchard's rather than Radcliffe-Brown's conception of anthropology that is embodied in a textbook published twenty years ago by another Oxford anthropologist, John Beattie. This book, entitled *Other Cultures*[17], was widely acclaimed on publication and is used as a text in introductory courses on anthropology throughout Britain and elsewhere. In it Beattie maintains that, although closely related to sociology, social anthropology is also different from it, for social anthropologists study 'other people's belief systems not simply from a sociological point of view, but also as being worthy of investigation in their own right'.[18]

Both Radcliffe-Brown and Evans-Pritchard emphasized fieldwork as a central part of anthropology, but their attitudes to fieldwork were nevertheless different. Radcliffe-Brown regarded fieldwork in the spirit of a natural scientist: for him the field was a kind of substitute for the laboratory. For Evans-Pritchard fieldwork was much more of a total experience with emotional as well as intellectual implications. It was like a journey into another world whose moral categories were exciting precisely because they were different. For

---

[15] For the British point of view see R. Firth, 'Contemporary British Social Anthropology', *American Anthropologist*, Vol. 53, 1951, pp. 474–90; for the American point of view see G. P. Murdock, 'British Social Anthropology', *American Anthropologist*, Vol. 53, 1951, pp. 465–73.

[16] Mayer Fortes has given a more differentiated account of the influences that contributed to the formation of British social anthropology: 'two distinct lines of descent are represented in the intellectual heritage of modern social anthropology. I see one as going back through Radcliffe-Brown, Lowie, and Rivers, to Morgan and Maine in particular, and the other as going back through Kroeber, Malinowski, and Frazer, to Tylor and to some extent Boas. I see the first one as the source of our structural concepts and theories, the second as the source of our speciality in the study of the facts of custom, or culture' (M. Fortes, *Kinship and the Social Order*, London: Routledge and Kegan Paul, 1970, p. 14). See also his *Social Anthropology in Cambridge since 1900*, Cambridge University Press, 1953.

[17] John Beattie, *Other Cultures*, Cohen and West, 1964.

[18] Ibid., p. 29.

Evans-Pritchard—and countless others—it was the challenge of coming to terms with an unfamiliar moral universe that gave zest to fieldwork and hence to anthropology.[19]

Evans-Pritchard has written memorably about his own fieldwork among the Nuer. 'I was a *ger*, what they call a *rul*, an alien sojourner, among them for only a year, but it was a year's relationship of great intensity, and the quality of a relationship counts for more than its duration.' It was, he said, 'an experience which has greatly influenced my life'.[20] One carries back something of the culture one experiences in the field but, of course, one leaves the people behind. It will be difficult to exaggerate the value placed by anthropologists like Evans-Pritchard on leaving unchanged—perhaps 'unspoilt' would be a better phrase—the people whose experiences they have shared during fieldwork.

The intellectual task to which primacy is assigned in the approach described above is the 'effort at translation'.[21] It is not enough to penetrate the moral universe of another culture. One must travel back into one's own universe and illuminate it with the insight gained by looking at the human condition from a different angle. This kind of anthropology presumes the unity of human beings, but it combines that presumption with a respect for their differences.

The same conception of anthropology as the study of other cultures, even remote cultures, has been articulated by its most celebrated living exponent, Claude Lévi-Strauss. '*The anthropologist*', he has said, using a striking phrase, '*is the astronomer of the social sciences*'.[22] The point of emphasis in this conception is that the societies studied by anthropologists are chosen not for their simplicity or even their primitiveness, but for their distance, their remoteness from the social universe of the anthropologist.[23]

Lévi-Strauss has claimed for the study of primitive societies a privileged status among the sciences of man.[24] This privileged status is claimed not by virtue of any intrinsic property of these societies

---

[19] The problems posed by an unfamiliar moral and intellectual universe are vividly documented in the first major study published by Evans-Pritchard, *Witchcraft, Oracles and Magic among the Azande*, Clarendon Press, 1937.

[20] E. E. Evans-Pritchard, *Nuer Religion*, Clarendon Press, 1956, p. ix.

[21] E. E. Evans-Pritchard, *Social Anthropology*, Cohen and West, 1951; see also Beattie, *Other Cultures*.

[22] C. Lévi-Strauss, *Structural Anthropology*, Penguin Books, 1977, p. 25.

[23] Ibid., p. 347.

[24] C. Lévi-Strauss, *Structural Anthropology 2*, Penguin Books, 1978, p. 25.

but by virtue of their position in relation to the observer: it is, as he puts it, 'the privilege of being distant'.[25] Distance not only gives enchantment to fieldwork, it provides a genuine advantage in the construction of theory. It is on this basis that Lévi-Strauss has repeatedly stressed the distinction between anthropology and sociology, and between anthropology and history.

The view from a distance has moral as well as scientific implications. The moral predicament of the anthropologist is different from that of the sociologist since the former studies societies other than his own whereas the latter studies his own society. 'The sociologist objectifies for fear of being misled. The ethnologist does not experience this fear since the distant society he studies *is nothing to him*, and since he is not compelled in advance to extract all its nuances, all its details, and even its values; in a word, all that in which the observer of his own society risks being implicated.'[26]

It is difficult to believe that the statement that the distant society the anthropologist studies 'is nothing to him' was meant to be taken literally. This was hardly Evans-Pritchard's sentiment about the Nuer, and I doubt if many anthropologists will subscribe to such a statement. On the contrary, they are inclined to stress the depth and intensity of their involvement with the people they have studied. If this appears at times to be a little strained, there is an element of generosity in it which it would be wrong to overlook.

While it is not generally true that the society studied by the anthropologist 'is nothing to him', it is nevertheless the case that anthropologists are on the whole reluctant to pass judgment on the societies they study. The moral attitude favoured by the anthropologist is not of the judge but of the witness. But this is an aspect of the relationship between the social scientist and the subject he studies that has received far less attention than it deserves. There has not been among anthropologists anything comparable to the debate among sociologists on the possibility of a value-free science of society. Perhaps there is at this level a genuine difference between those who study their own society and those who study other cultures.

Marxism as the Philosophy of Praxis

It is not necessary to argue at length that there are several versions of Marxism, indeed, several versions of orthodox

[25] Ibid., p. 28.
[26] Ibid., p. 26, emphasis added.

Marxism.[27] Marxism has been presented as positive science and as revolutionary dialectic, as historical materialism and as philosophy of praxis. It is not my intention here either to attempt to reconcile these or other versions of Marxism or to argue that such an attempt at reconciliation is bound to fail. My aim is to discover where the points of tension between Marxism and anthropology lie, and if I choose to dwell on a particular version of Marxism, I do so with that aim in view.

All Marxists have assigned some importance to the connexion between Marxism as an intellectual system with its own concepts and categories and Marxism as a political movement with its own aims and objectives.[28] After pointing to the fact that the founding of the First International and the publication of the first volume of *Capital* took place within three years of each other, Karl Korsch wrote, 'Within one single period of history, in the 1860s, both aspects of Marxism attained their full realization: the new autonomous science of the working class attained its developed theoretical form in literature at the same time as the new autonomous movement of the proletariat achieved its practical form in history'.[29] Marxists like Korsch and Lukács insisted that this connexion was necessary and not contingent, and they saw in it the real foundation of their own method—the dialectical method—as against the methods of bourgeois social science.

If we speak today of a Marxist economics, a Marxist sociology, and even a Marxist anthropology, this is because Marxism has had a strong sense of its identity as an alternative to and not merely a critique of 'bourgeois' social science. This sense of Marxism as a radical alternative—a completely new departure—has not been equally strong everywhere or at all times, but it has given a distinctive orientation to Marxism as an intellectual system. We must proceed with some awareness of this if we are to explore the possibility of bringing together Marxism and anthropology, a discipline which has grown largely since Marx's time and outside the framework of his thought.

---

[27] See Ch. 7.

[28] Firth's distinction between 'gut-Marxists' and 'cerebral Marxists' might appeal to a certain kind of common sense, but it is not likely to be acceptable to Marxists themselves. See Raymond Firth, *The Sceptical Anthropologist? Social Anthropology and Marxist Views on Society*, The British Academy, 1972.

[29] Karl Korsch, *Marxism and Philosophy*, Monthly Review, 1970, p. 171.

Marx presented his own principal work as a 'critique of political economy', intending it as a critique of both a given order of reality and a given body of theory. The theory was in some sense a reflection of the reality and its limitation lay precisely in its inability to see the contradictions in the reality of which it was a reflection. The categories of bourgeois thought were the categories of bourgeois society, and political economists from Petty to Ricardo had assumed these categories to be absolute, eternal and unchanging. Therefore, the critique of political economy could be made from only a particular standpoint, the standpoint of 'the class whose vocation in history is the overthrow of the capitalist mode of production and the final abolition of all classes—the proletariat'.[30]

The view of Marxism as an alternative to bourgeois social science, if not a negation of it, gained ground after Marx's death, especially after the great success of the Bolshevik revolution. Such a view was for a time sought to be extended to all branches of learning, although it could not be pressed equally far in the physical as in the historical sciences. It is not surprising that sociology was virtually supplanted during the whole of Stalin's regime; ethnography, however, was allowed to function within its particular sphere.

Marx's penetrating insights into the complex relationship between categories of thought and modes of social existence became codified into somewhat mechanical formulas in the hands of Soviet Marxists.[31] One such formula related to the 'class character of the social sciences'. In an influential work first published in 1921, N. I. Bukharin, then in the front rank of Soviet Marxist intellectuals, wrote, 'It is not difficult to see that bourgeois practice will demand one thing, and proletarian practice another; that the bourgeoisie will have one view of things and the working class another; that the social science of the bourgeoisie will be of one type, and that of the proletariat unquestionably of a different type'.[32] Bukharin's didactic style is characteristic; what is unusual, for at least that phase in Soviet intellectual life, is his attempt to develop a system of sociology within the framework of historical materialism.[33]

[30] Karl Marx, *Capital*, Progress Publishers, 1954, Vol. 1, pp. 25–6.
[31] See my *Marxism, Pluralism and Orthodoxy*.
[32] Nikolai Bukharin, *Historical Materialism, A System of Sociology*, University of Michigan Press, 1969, p. 11.
[33] Soviet Marxism remained indifferent, not to say hostile, to sociology until the mid-1950s.

While all social knowledge was believed in principle to have a class basis, not all the social sciences were viewed as being governed equally by class. For a variety of historical reasons, sociology was singled out as representing the standpoint of the bourgeoisie.[34] Economics and ethnography were viewed in a somewhat different light, the former because it was thought to have some of the properties of the natural sciences, and the latter because it was thought to be not directly involved in the interests of either of the two basic classes. The distinction between sociology and anthropology (or ethnography, to use the Soviet phrase) in Soviet social science is rooted in the distinction, fundamental to Soviet Marxism, between 'class societies' and 'classless societies'.

The view that social theory is or ought to be rooted in practical activity became quickly stereotyped within Soviet Marxism. But the same view served to breathe new life into Marxism outside the Soviet Union, particularly in the writings of Korsch, Lukács and Gramsci who were all contemporaries of Bukharin. All three writers had been deeply impressed by the Bolshevik revolution and they all sought, against the orthodoxy of the Second International, to present a version of Marxism that would acknowledge its profound significance for theory as well as practice.

Korsch and Lukács stressed the inherently revolutionary character of Marxism as both scientific theory and political movement: 'The philosophers have only *interpreted* the world, in various ways; the point is to *change* it'.[35] For them Marxism viewed as a positive science whose truth was independent of any political struggle was a contradiction in terms. A certain conception of Marxism as a positive science, more objective, more comprehensive and more accurate than previous forms of it, had become established as a part of the orthodoxy of the Second International. Korsch, Lukács and others attacked this conception as being a denial of the spirit of Marxism which was 'dialectical in theory and revolutionary in practice'[36].

The link between Marxist theory and the revolutionary movement of the proletariat is an internal one. The theory cannot be fabricated

---

[34] The roots of this go back to Plekhanov's antipathy to Mikhailovsky and, beyond that, to Marx's dismissive attitude to Comte.

[35] The eleventh and last of Marx's celebrated *Theses on Feuerbach*.

[36] Korsch, *Marxism and Philosophy*, p. 69. It was precisely from this point of view that Goldmann had questioned the possibility of a Marxist sociology in 'Y a-t-il une sociologie marxiste?'

independently of the movement at one place and applied at another place to the creation of such a movement. As Korsch put it, 'The emergence of Marxist theory is, in Hegelian-Marxist terms, only the "other side" of the emergence of the real proletarian movement; it is both sides together that comprise the concrete totality of the historical process'.[37] It is not easy to see how this can accommodate the kind of intellectual endeavour which defines itself as the study of societies at a distance.

Korsch made the mistake of attacking in the name of Marxism both Kautsky and Lenin, and his work soon faded from view. But the idea of Marxism as the theoretical expression of the revolutionary movement of the proletariat lived on in the writings of Georg Lukács whose towering intellectual personality haunted European Marxists of more than one generation. I must say at once that I am not concerned here with the correct interpretation of Lukács's entire work which underwent many transformations[38], but only with a particular vision of Marxism which has been expressed over and over again, but never as forcefully, as exactly or as clearly as by him.

As is well known, Lukács sought to characterise Marxism not by its results but by its method. He refused to make any concession to the criticisms of the revisionists and he rejected at the same time the orthodoxy of the Second International. He castigated those Marxists, whether 'revisionist' or 'orthodox' who 'seek refuge in the methods of natural science, in the way in which science distills 'pure' facts and places them in the relevant contexts by means of observation, abstraction and experiment'.[39] Thus, 'method' for Lukács meant something quite different from the methods of fact-finding developed by bourgeois social scientists in imitation of the natural sciences.[40]

The method characteristic of Marxism is the dialectic which is a movement towards unity of subject and object. Thought must change, but so must reality: 'It is not enough that thought should

---

[37] Korsch, *Marxism and Philosophy*, p. 45.

[38] The changes of position adopted by Lukács have been written about by many, including Lukács himself. For a brief summary, see George Lichtheim, *Lukács*, Fontana/Collins, 1970. See also his own 'Preface to the New Edition (1967)' in Georg Lukács, *History and Class Consciousness*, Merlin Press, 1971.

[39] Ibid., p. 5.

[40] Ibid. See also Jean-Paul Sartre, *The Problem of Method*, Methuen, 1963.

seek to realise itself; reality must also strive towards thought'.[41] Again, as Lukács puts it, 'for the dialectical method the central problem is to *change reality*'.[42] The dialectic is the appropriate method in the human sciences because the understanding of reality can be achieved only in the process of changing it.

The dialectical method is defined by Lukács in the sharpest opposition to the method of contemplation. Much of what passes for science in the bourgeois world, including natural science with its experimental method, is pure contemplation, for it accepts the structure of the world as it is given. Marxism rejects the possibility of understanding through pure contemplation. Nor is it a question of rejecting it only in theory. One must change the world through rational practical action; or else accept it blindly, fatalistically and without comprehension. Perhaps few Marxists would carry the argument about the dialectical unity of theory and practice to the point to which it was taken by Lukács; yet it cannot be denied that there is a fundamental antipathy in Marxism of every variety towards a contemplative orientation to the world.

The idea of Marxism as practical activity rather than disinterested pursuit of knowledge finds its most authentic expression in the life and work of Gramsci. Gramsci's description of Marxism as 'philosophy of praxis' was meant to evade the censors, but it was also singularly appropriate to his conception of it. Others have used the phrase 'critical philosophy', but for Gramsci the practical or creative side of Marxism was as important as the critical.

There are certain aspects of Gramsci's approach which the anthropologist is likely to find particularly congenial. These include his deep and continued preoccupation with culture, and his rejection of a one-sided emphasis on economic and material factors. An important reason behind the apathy if not the hostility of most anthropologists towards Marxism has been the close historical association of Marxism with economic determinism, and its relative neglect of culture as an important and to some extent autonomous area of collective life. In his effort to free Marxism from the strait-jacket of a materialist philosophy, Gramsci appears to give back to culture its due place in human life.

Gramsci's concern, however, was not with culture at a distance

[41] Karl Marx, *The Critique of Hegel's Philosophy of Right* in T. B. Bottomore (ed.), *Karl Marx: Early Writings*, C. A. Watts, 1963, p. 54.
[42] Lukács, *History and Class Consciousness*, p. 3.

but with culture at close quarters. The philosophy of praxis would cease to be itself if it became absorbed in a detached contemplation of distant cultures without any practical aim in relation to those cultures. Gramsci believed that a new culture representing the life and aspirations of a new class was taking birth and that the philosophy of praxis had a part to play in understanding it and, above all, in creating it.

Gramsci maintained that capitalism exercised pre-eminence not only in politics but also in thought. Capitalism could be displaced only by a new civilization which could not be called into being by a mere change in the distribution of power. What was required above all was a new way of looking at the world, new ideas and beliefs, in short, a new culture. It is here that the philosophy of praxis had a pre-eminent role 'as a modern popular reformation'.[43] The philosophy of praxis has aims and objectives that are distinct from those of any of the specialized social sciences.

The intellectual content, and not merely the intellectual function, of the philosophy of praxis is inseparable from the life of the class and party which are its characteristic bearers. Marxism not only expresses and creates the world-view of the working class, it can grow as an intellectual system only within the framework of the working-class party. The party rather than the detached or independent scholar was to provide intellectual leadership to the people. Marxism as the philosophy of praxis would reduce itself to nullity in isolating itself from the working-class movement and its political organ.

The distinctiveness of Marxism lies not so much in its rejection of a value-neutral science of society and culture as in the way in which its intellectual enterprise has been linked, in Marx's own writings, with the working-class movement, and, since Lenin's time, with the working-class party. Perhaps Marxism itself is now entering a new phase, as it did in 1889 with the establishment of the Second International, when these concerns were to some extent displaced by other ones. But even under the Second International they were only displaced and never repudiated or rejected.

Soviet and Western Anthropology

The fact that the philosophy of praxis may not go very well with the study of society at a distance does not necessarily mean that

[43] Antonio Gramsci, *Selections from Prison Notebooks*, Lawrence and Wishart, 1971, p. 395.

Marxists must neglect anthropology or that anthropologists should be indifferent to Marxism. Various kinds of accommodation have in fact been achieved and maintained between anthropology and Marxism at different times and in different places. It will be impossible to assess fully the relationship between Marxism and anthropology without considering some of the attempts so far made to develop a Marxist anthropology.[44]

Marxism had made very little impact on Western anthropology until about twenty years ago. Maurice Godelier says, 'Marxism only made its appearance in anthropological research in France some time around the 1960s'.[45] In Britain there were occasional attempts to apply the materialist interpretation of history to primitive societies, as in Peter Worsley's ill-fated Curle Bequest Prize Essay[46], but these were few and far between.[47] The situation was not very different in the United States although there the work of Leslie White and his associates created some interest in what came to be known later as 'cultural materialism'.[48] Otherwise, if anthropologists from these countries ever referred to Marx and Engels, it was generally to show that almost everything the latter had written in *The Origin of the Family, Private Property and the State* was factually wrong and theoretically unsound.

When we turn to the Soviet Union we get a different picture. Soviet ethnography and Western anthropology developed along somewhat different paths, and while Marxism is only now beginning to find adherents in the West, it has provided an intellectual background for ethnographic studies in the Soviet Union from the very beginning. Soviet scholars have maintained the distinction between

[44] See, for instance, Maurice Bloch (ed.), *Marxist Analyses and Social Anthropology*, Malaby Press, 1975; see also his *Marxism and Anthropology*.

[45] Maurice Godelier, 'The Emergence and Development of Marxism in Anthropology in France' in Ernest Gellner (ed.), *Soviet and Western Anthropology*, New York: Columbia University Press, 1980, p. 3. See also his *Perspectives in Marxist Anthropology*, Cambridge University Press, 1977 (first published in French, 1973).

[46] P. M. Worsley, 'The Kinship System of the Tallensi: a Revaluation', *Journal of the Royal Anthropological Institute*, Vol. 86, 1956, pp. 37–75; see also n. 62 below.

[47] M. N. Srinivas has pointed out in a personal communication the interest taken in the 1940s by both Gluckman and Fortes in some of the ideas of Marx, but even Gluckman's approach to these ideas was eclectic. The first recent attempt by a major British anthropologist to review the relationship between the two was in Raymond Firth's Inaugural Radcliffe-Brown Lecture in 1972; see n. 28 above.

[48] See Marvin Harris, *Cultural Materialism, The Struggle for a Science of Culture*, Random House, 1979.

sociology and ethnography (i.e. anthropology) even more clearly than their Western counterparts, and while sociology suffered long neglect, ethnography was able to follow a more even course of development. In no sense did ethnography seek to present itself as an alternative to Marxism, as bourgeois sociology might appear to have done.

Soviet ethnographers, like Western anthropologists, began with the study of primitive, pre-literate or simple societies. The ethnographers were the first experts on the races, languages and cultures of the simpler peoples, but for various historical reasons the distinction between the study of other cultures and of one's own society did not acquire the same form in the Soviet Union as it did in America and Europe. Soviet ethnography is now extending its scope to cover all social formations from the simplest to the most complex[49], but even here its subject matter, the study of ethnos and ethnicos[50], reflects strikingly its basic pre-occupation with pre-class societies.

To the extent that Soviet ethnography has grown within the climate of Soviet Marxism, it has been marked by its emphasis on materialism and on progress, of which the cause as well as the symptom is material progress. In this sense Soviet ethnography has retained much more of the original flavour of anthropology as it was in the nineteenth century than its counterparts in Europe and America. The link with the nineteenth century goes through Engels to Morgan and the beginnings of anthropology. Nineteenth-century anthropology, including the anthropology of Morgan, was evolutionary rather than revolutionary. The connexion between what Engels wrote about primitive societies and any kind of revolutionary praxis was at best indirect and implicit.

The two outstanding features of Soviet ethnography as I see it are its historicist concern and its concern with the problems of ethnos.[51] Both these have been fitted into the framework of Marxism which in the Soviet Union is viewed above all as the materialist interpretation of history. If Soviet ethnographers show greater unity in their theoretical framework than their Western counterparts, this is partly because of the high degree of consistency characteristic of Soviet Marxism. This is not to say that there are no disagreements among

---

[49] See Gellner (ed.), *Soviet and Western Anthropology*, part 3, especially the contributions by Y. Bromley and L. Drobizheva.   [50] Ibid.

[51] Ibid., especially the articles by Y. Petrova-Averikieva and by Y. Bromley.

Soviet ethnographers, but these disagreements centre around certain basic issues whose significance is widely, if not universally, acknowledged.

A statement by a Soviet ethnographer declares; 'The leading principle of ethnographic research in the U.S.S.R. is historicism'; and further, 'The Marxist materialistic view of history underlies this approach'.[52] Soviet ethnography has, in keeping with the spirit of Soviet Marxism, served to reinforce the view that human history is an extension of natural history. Not only is progress ineluctable, but the stages of progress are also determinate, and one of the tasks of ethnography is to identify the succession of stages in the development of society.[53]

The concept of ethnos has provided Soviet ethnographers with their basic organizing principle for studying the contemporary world. Indeed, it is through the development of this concept and its application to the contemporary world that Soviet ethnography has made its most significant advances. The concept of ethnos has enabled Soviet ethnographers to study all social formations from the most archaic to the most progressive within a single theoretical framework. It has enabled them to reach towards a universal human problem while articulating at the same time a distinctively Soviet preoccupation. Soviet ethnography has not only had greater continuity than Soviet sociology, it has also been more innovative.

It would, however, be a mistake to overlook the fact that the concern for ethnos derives from the historical association between ethnography and the study of archaic or simple societies. Thus, while the division of labour between ethnography and sociology no longer rests on the simple distinction between archaic and progressive societies, a division of labour nevertheless exists. This division of labour rests on the distinction between 'ethnic' phenomena and 'social' phenomena in the strict sense of the term. As a leading Soviet ethnographer has put it, 'It is necessary to note the conventional delimitation of ethnic phenomena proper and social phenomena proper; by the latter we understand essentially class and professional relations and corresponding institutions'.[54] In other

[52] Y. Petrova-Averikieva, 'Historicism in Soviet Ethnographic Science' in Gellner (ed.), *Soviet and Western Anthropology*, p. 19.

[53] See in particular the contributions by Y. I. Semenov and E. Gellner in Gellner (ed.), *Soviet and Western Anthropology*.

[54] Y. Bromley, 'The Object and the Subject-matter of Ethnography' in Gellner (ed.), *Soviet and Western Anthropology*, p. 155.

words, the study of class is put outside the reach of ethnography by confining the latter to the study of either 'pre-class' societies in their totality or ethnos and ethnicos in 'class' and 'post-class' societies.

In fairness to Soviet social science, it must be pointed out that the concerns of Soviet Marxism, at least since the death of Lenin, have never been the same as the concerns of Occidental Marxism.[55] Soviet Marxism has presented itself as dialectical materialism rather than as philosophy of praxis, and its concerns have been those of a post-Revolutionary society, i.e., one in which the working-class revolution has already been made. Hence the kinds of tension on which I have earlier dwelt are likely to be least marked in Soviet ethnography, especially since Soviet ethnographers have never ventured on field expeditions outside their own society extensively enough to have felt the need to claim a separate scientific status for the study of other cultures.

When we turn to the West, we are struck by the diversity of both Western anthropology and Western Marxism. The conception of Marxism as a philosophy of praxis and of anthropology as the study of other cultures are both distinctively Western conceptions, but this does not mean that either conception has held its ground without any rival. Indeed, most Western anthropologists who have thought of themselves as Marxists have thought of Marxism somewhat differently from the way in which Lukács or Gramsci might represent it. For them the main lesson to be drawn from Marxism has been materialism rather than the unity of theory and practice. They have, with a few exceptions, fought shy of the problem of relating their theoretical enterprise to any kind of political practice within a Marxist framework.

In discussing the interface between Marxism and Western anthropology I shall speak first of American anthropology and then of British and French anthropology. American anthropology had for a long time a place for a few Marxists, although it was a subordinate place. The mainstream of American anthropology has at least since the time of Boas been either unsympathetic or indifferent to most if

---

[55] I have discussed the hiatus between Soviet and Occidental Marxism in my M. N. Roy Memorial Lecture cited above (n. 27). But there is a vast literature on the subject to which a recent contribution has been made by Perry Anderson, *Considerations on Western Marxism*, London: New Left Books, 1976. For a more extended discussion, see Leszek Kolakowski, *Main Currents of Marxism*, Clarendon Press, 1978, 3 Vols., especially Vol. 3.

not all of the concerns of Marxism. Until the 1960s and 1970s Marxist anthropologists in America were a small minority, sharing perhaps a certain sense of being victims of the academic establishment.[56]

The mainstream of American anthropology has been dominated at least in the present century by its anti-evolutionist bias and by its concern for culture viewed as the superorganic. The former may be traced back to Boas[57] and the latter was given currency by Kroeber.[58] On both these counts Marxist anthropologists came into conflict with established positions in their discipline. For some time it was mainly the Marxists who were prepared to champion the theory of evolution although, of course, there is no necessary connexion between Marxism and evolutionism, the concept of evolution fitting better in most ways with a liberal than a radical theory of history.[59] Further, it became a hallmark of the Marxist approach to primitive societies to stress the primacy of material factors over beliefs and values, although, again, material culture had at one time been a subject of general interest for all anthropologists.

The American anthropologist known best for his Marxist sympathies was Leslie White who exercised considerable influence through his own work and the work of his younger colleagues and pupils at the University of Michigan. Leslie White was an evolutionist and a materialist, perhaps best known for his 'energy theory of culture', according to which the evolution of culture may be measured by the amount of energy harnessed per capita per annum.[60]

It was Leslie White who developed the viewpoint known as 'cultural materialism', although the term itself was given currency by Marvin Harris who became best known among White's successors

[56] This sense is very clearly expressed by Marvin Harris in his massive work, *The Rise of Anthropological Theory*, New York: Crowell, 1968, although it is not very easy to assess the objective basis of this feeling of persecution.

[57] The anti-evolutionist bias in Boas is well known. For an assessment of his work by a leading American evolutionist, see Leslie A. White, *The Ethnography and Ethnology of Franz Boas*, Bulletin of the Texas Memorial Museum, no. 6, Austin, Texas, 1963.

[58] A. L. Kroeber, *The Nature of Culture*, Chicago: University of Chicago Press, 1952. The phrase itself goes back to Herbert Spencer.

[59] The connexion between evolutionism and the liberal view of history was traced by Mannheim in several of his writings. See Karl Mannheim, *Ideology and Utopia*, London: Routledge and Kegan Paul, 1936; also his *Essays on Sociology and Social Psychology*, Routledge and Kegan Paul, 1953.

[60] Leslie A. White, *The Science of Culture*, Farrar, Strauss, 1969.

for his Marxist sympathies.[61] But cultural materialism, whether in White's conception of it or in the form given to it by Harris, is Marxism in only a very special sense. Both White and Harris reject the dialectic as an unnecessary obstacle to the development of a scientific cultural anthropology. Harris in particular has argued for a value-neutral anthropology, maintaining that cultural materialism has no implications for political practice.

British anthropology had until the 1970s maintained a comfortable distance from Marxism, although some might detect a Marxist aroma in the work of Gluckman and more recently in that of Goody. A notable exception in the fifties was the ambitious paper by P. M. Worsley which sought to recast Fortes's Tallensi material within a Marxist framework.[62] This framework had at that time appeared fairly simple and straightforward in that it was based on a recognition of the primacy of the relations of production (meaning the economic structure) over the superstructure (including kinship). Worsley took his stand on the argument that the primacy of economics over kinship, which had been established in the study of advanced societies, was in fact valid for all societies. Although he was a committed Marxist when he wrote his paper, Worsley did not spell out the political implications for the Tallensi of his new theoretical insight into their social structure.

There is today much greater interest among British social anthropologists in modes of production.[63] This interest has impelled them to take a closer look at the entire corpus of Marx's writings rather than at only those which Marx, and more particularly Engels, devoted to non-Western societies.[64] Though central to the Marxist approach, an interest in modes of production does not of course commit an anthropologist to Marxism as a system. One may well consider a society's mode of production to be only one among its several fundamental features, and an interest in modes of production may or may not be accompanied by a commitment to any specific programme of action. All that can be said perhaps is that

[61] Harris, *The Rise of Anthropological Theory*.

[62] P. M. Worsley, 'The Kinship System of the Tallensi: A Revaluation'. Fortes has disposed of Worsley's argument in his outstanding work, *Kinship and the Social Order*, pp. 220 ff. But see also Marshall Sahlins, *Culture and Practical Reason*, University of Chicago Press, 1976, pp. 4–18.

[63] See, for instance, Bloch (ed.), *Marxist Analyses and Social Anthropology*: also his *Marxism and Anthropology*, especially chapter 6.

[64] Bloch, *Marxism and Anthropology*.

anthropologists in Britain have shed some of their inhibitions about appropriating concepts believed earlier to have been tainted by their association with Marxism.

The interest among British anthropologists in modes of production owes much to influences from France which is the only country outside the U.S.S.R. where serious attempts are being made to establish a fully-formed Marxist anthropology. French anthropology differs from Soviet ethnography as much as French Marxism does from Soviet Marxism, but beyond that it is not easy to say much more. French anthropology has attained international standing relatively recently and French Marxist anthropology even more recently, and it is still marked by something of the effervescence of a new intellectual movement. Almost from its very birth Marxist anthropology in France has been divided, and this very division reveals some of the fundamental problems that arise in bringing Marxism and anthropology face to face.

Maurice Godelier, a leading exponent of French Marxist anthropology, has listed the principal issues that divide Marxist anthropologists in France.[65] These include issues of both theory and practice, but, while he has dwelt at some length on questions of theory, he has barely touched upon the political issues involved. We learn that some French Marxist anthropologists are or were Trotskyist activists and others Communist Party activists, but we do not learn what implications this has for the communities they investigate.[66] Anthropological investigation, of no matter what kind, obviously has some direct implications for the investigators; one presumes that a truly Marxist investigation would also have some implications for the investigated.

We get some indication of the way in which Marxist anthropology can relate to the political concerns of the people under investigation in the work of Claude Meillassoux.[67] Beginning with studies in West Africa, he has tried to show how capitalism sucks the tribal domestic community into its orbit of influence. Deprived of hearth and home, the West African tribesman or peasant becomes a migrant labourer in France where he has to work under severely exploitative conditions. The peasant-proletarian from

---

[65] See n. 45.   [66] Ibid., pp. 3–5.

[67] Claude Meillassoux, *Maidens, Meal and Money*, Cambridge: Cambridge University Press, 1981 (first published in French in 1975); see also his *Anthropologie economique des Gouro de Cote d'Ivoire*, Mouton, 1964.

West Africa lives in two worlds without security in either. Meillassoux's work on tribal migrants moving between West Africa and France is as yet tentative and exploratory, but it seems to me to be based on an implicit rejection of the idea that anthropology is the study of other cultures and that the anthropologist is the astronomer of the social sciences.

Marxism as a theory of knowledge is concerned in a fundamental way with the practical implications of that knowledge for the people whose lives it seeks to illuminate. Knowledge about the Nuer is not just for the anthropologist; it is, or should be, above all, for the Nuer: to compromise on this would be to repudiate the spirit of Marxism. It seems to me that although many Western anthropologists are today captivated by Marxism, few have given serious thought to the part that may be played by the knowledge they generate in transforming the lives of the people among whom they live and work as anthropologists. Their political concerns, if any, have been mainly with the implications for themselves of political divisions in their home environment.

A question on which Marxists and non-Marxists are often divided in the related field of sociology is that of a value-neutral science of society.[68] At least in Western countries today the idea of a value-neutral sociology is associated more with a non-Marxist or bourgeois point of view, whereas most Marxists would maintain that such a sociology is neither possible nor desirable.[69] The place of values in the study of culture and society has not been discussed in quite the same terms in anthropology as in sociology, although the question is as important in the one case as in the other. The possibility of a distinctively Marxist anthropology will, in my opinion, turn much more around this question than around questions about modes of production or the relationship between infrastructure and superstructure.

[68] I have discussed some of these questions in my *Ideologies and Intellectuals*, Oxford University Press, 1980.

[69] I do not wish to overdraw the contrast. The influential group of Marxists, known as Austro-Marxists, acknowledged the possibility of a value-free science of society—and were duly attacked by Korsch, Goldmann, etc. For the Austro-Marxist viewpoint, see Otto Neurath, *Empiricism and Sociology*, Dordrecht (The Netherlands): Reidel, 1973; see also T. Bottomore and P. Goode (eds), *Austro-Marxism*, Clarendon Press, 1978. On the other side, not all non-Marxists have or claim to have a value-free approach to the study of society and culture.

Those with a liberal conscience are perhaps inclined to feel that, while a case may be made for passing judgment on one's own society, it might be unethical or at least ungenerous to do the same for another society. A person is bound to his own society in a way in which he never is to a remote or a distant society. A recommendation for political intervention is never without a price. A person pays at least part of the price of his recommendation for his own society: who pays the price of one's recommendation for another society?

As is well known, the assessment among Marxists of the revolutionary potential of the different parts of the world has altered vastly between the time of Marx's death and the present. Marx and his immediate successors thought of the advanced societies of the West—England, France and Germany—when they thought of a revolutionary transformation through the class struggle. The countries of Asia, Latin America and Africa did not figure very prominently in their consideration of the centres of revolutionary movements. If they thought of hunters, gatherers and shifting cultivators, they thought of them as objects rather than as subjects of history.

All of this has changed in the hundred years since the death of Marx. The Bolshevik and the Chinese revolutions revealed the part that revolutionary consciousness could play in economically-backward societies. The withdrawal of the established imperial powers—Britain, France, the Netherlands—from their colonies was accompanied by revolutionary, militant and insurgent movements in Asia, Africa and Latin America. Precisely at that historical moment when the working-class movement in the West faced the threat of embourgeoisement, the Third World was waking to new life, opening up unprecedented vistas of revolutionary possibility.

It is well known that in the 1960s radical movements in the West under the inspiration of writers ranging from Marcuse to Fanon turned their attention away from the established working class in search of revolutionary potential among new classes and strata. These included students, but also minorities, 'ethnics' and tribals—the very people whose study had been the anthropologist's vocation. It is difficult to believe that the appearance of Marxism in anthropological research in the 1960s, of which Godelier has spoken, was unrelated to the appearance at the same time of new possibilities of political mobilization. Needless to say, all of this made little or no impact on Marxist ethnography in the Soviet Union.

It is not surprising that anthropologists who leave their homes in Europe and North America to do fieldwork in distant places in Asia, Africa and Latin America are often struck by the material and moral impoverishment of the people among whom they live and work. Imperialism, capitalism and neo-colonialism have left very few parts of the world untouched, and 'the destruction of aboriginal society' has become a commonplace of anthropological writing. The same Lévi-Strauss who has called the anthropologist the 'astronomer of the social sciences' has also described anthropology as 'daughter of an era of violence'.[70]

More than any other social scientist from the West, it is the anthropologist who encounters at close quarters people of small resources whose very survival is threatened by the advance of civilization. The experience of fieldwork, which has become the hallmark of anthropological research, particularly in Britain, gives him a kind of privileged access to the inner lives of the people he studies. As has been stressed by so many practitioners of the craft, fieldwork is as much a moral as an intellectual experience. Whatever may be their general intellectual orientations, few anthropologists find it easy to adopt a morally-neutral position towards the people whose lives have, however briefly, touched their own.

Although the anthropologist seeks out an alien culture, he does so with the conscious intention of establishing a point of intimate contact with another human community. Anthropologists have written at length about the human aspects of their fieldwork experiences in distant places. Graduate seminars in Departments of Anthropology, at least in the English-speaking world, are full of personal accounts of each member's experience of his own fieldwork. It is almost a point of honour with the anthropologist to speak well and perhaps also to think well of his chosen people.[71]

Even where the anthropologist defines his theoretical task as the study of other cultures, it does not necessarily mean that he practices detachment from the community he actually studies. Anthropologists of every persuasion develop some kind of commitment to the well-being of these communities. It is not surprising that at least some of

---

[70] C. Lévi-Strauss, 'Anthropology: Its Achievements and Future', *Current Anthropology*, Vol. 7, no. 2, 1966, p. 126.

[71] There are no doubt exceptions. Among the ones better known are R. F. Fortune, *Sorcerers of Dobu*, London: Routledge and Kegan Paul, 1932, and Cora Dubois, *The People of Alor*, Harvard University Press, 1960.

them should seek to translate this commitment into a programme of social transformation based on a definite ideology. Perhaps this urge to generate a total political transformation has grown with the growing awareness of the misery and squalor that are the common lot of tribesmen and peasants in Asia, Africa and Latin America. Viewed in this light, Marxism appeals to something generous in the anthropologist as a person with a concern for the human condition.

But after all this has been said, it must also be admitted that there is an element of make-believe in the intimacy between the anthropologist and his chosen people. Nothing is more difficult than to establish true reciprocity between unequals; and having for twenty-five years watched Western anthropologists come to do fieldwork in India, I am not sure that all of them have even a genuine desire for reciprocity. The anthropologist comes with gifts which his informants covet even when they suspect that they may not be of much value. It is true that the anthropologist has to endure many of the hardships of a life of meagre resources. But his hardships are the hardships of camp life; the hardships of the natives are permanent and without visible escape.

Even where the moral concern of the anthropologist for the people he studies is deep and authentic, it does not follow that this concern will be expressed in a political programme. The lack of a definite political programme is no evidence of absence of concern, particularly where it is a question of another society. It will not be difficult to find examples where anthropologists have felt and expressed, at some risk to themselves, deep moral concern for the people they have studied without engaging in political action that might put at risk the people whose trust they have enjoyed.

Advocates of a Marxist anthropology must accept the full implications of the distinction between the anthropologist as witness and as partisan. Nothing much is required to be said about the anthropologist as witness because that has been his conventional role as a student of other cultures at least since the profession differentiated itself from the activities of explorers, missionaries and administrators. It is true that some anthropologists have in the past played a sort of political role as agents of the colonial government, but this is an aspect of their past of which liberal anthropologists are not very proud. If there are anthropologists today who continue to play such a role, they do so furtively and under cover of some other activity.

For a hundred years and more Marxists in Germany, France, Italy and other Western countries have debated and explored the possibilities of creating a scientific understanding of their own society in conjunction with the working-class movement. They have spoken of a new kind of intellectual—the 'organic' intellectual—and of a new milieu for intellectual activity—the working-class party—as bearers of a new understanding of society. Marxist anthropologists have not so far provided any significant clues as to how they expect to achieve the unity of theory and practice in their encounters with distant societies.

The Marxist anthropologist, if he is true to his political vocation, will resist the delimitation of anthropology to the study of other cultures. Those of us who have sought to resist this delimitation on other grounds have come to realise how difficult it is in practice to do so. Linking the study of man to a political project brings out another dimension of this difficulty. The anthropologist does not stand in the same relationship to the tribesmen he studies as the sociologist does to the working class in his own society. The man who combines science and politics in his own society accepts a lifelong commitment, exposing himself to all the risks of such a commitment. The anthropologist who goes to work in a distant community is by contrast a transient, what the French call a *passager*: he can give only a small part of himself and therefore his claims will always remain suspect. In this sense a Marxist anthropology appears to be even more problematic than a Marxist sociology.

Production, mode of, 119, 160–1
Proletariat, 150–1; rural, 95
Protective discrimination, 77

Radcliffe-Brown, A.R., 2, 3, 5, 11, 17, 19, 143–6
Raiyat, 70
Raj Gond, 69, 71–2
Rajput, 53, 54, 58, 68, 74, 86
Rampura, 38, 43, 54
Redfield, R., 27–30, 39, 40, 43, 44, 47–51, 62, 112
Revisionism, 132, 133
Revolutionary prophylaxis, 26
Ricardo, D., 150
Rivers, W.H.R., 8, 14, 15, 146n
Rodinson, M., 118, 139
Roy, S.C., 69, 70, 73
Russell, B., 123

Sadgope, 54
Sahlins, M.D., 17n, 63, 78, 79, 81n, 161n
Sanskritization, 56
Santal, 18, 44, 63, 66–8, 73–6
Sartre, J.-P., 108, 126n, 128, 129, 152n
Savara, 75
Second International, 129, 133, 136, 151, 152, 154
Segmentary system, 63–4, 76, 78, 79
Semenov, Y.I., 157n
Sen, S., 99
Shamirpet, 37
Shanin, T., 26, 48, 49, 51, 66, 67
Shifting cultivation, 72, 76
Shirokogoroff, S.M., 32
Sils, D.L., 46n, 63n, 93n, 142n
Simirenko, A., 103n
Singer, M., 30, 62n
Sinha, S., 61n, 62n
Smith, R.E.F., 26n
Smith, R.S., 64n
Social anthropology, as comparative sociology, 144; as comparative study of human societies, 142; Chinese, 3; relationship with sociology, 4–5, 12, 101; study of primitive, pre-literate or tribal societies, 5, 7, 10, 60, 145

Social: fact, 4; formation, 119; morphology, 145; philosophy, 5, 104; structure, 145; transformation, 105
Socialism, 134; scientific, 123, 134
Sociology, 1, 2, 104, 107–8, 151; American, 3, 4, 7, 8, 10 and ethnology, 13, 15; and ethnosociology, 20–2; as 'auxiliary discipline', 108; as value-neutral science, 162; bourgeois, 3, 103; Chinese, 31, distinction between Marxist and bourgeois, 104; European, 102; French, 103; German, 3; in Britain, 10; rural, 7; Soviet, 3, 4, 103–4
Solzhenitsyn, A., 123n
Srinivas, M.N., 3n, 17, 38, 39n, 56, 143n, 155n
Sripuram, 51–4
Stalin, J.V., 114, 122, 126, 127n, 135, 138, 139, 150
Stalinism, 116
Stalinist, 124, 138
Status situation, 93
Superstructure, 108, 161, 162; and contradictions within the base, 110; distinction between 'basic structure' and, 110; relation between base and, 104, 123, 126–7
Survey research, 10
Suye Mura, 61

Tagore, R., 31
Taitou, 33
Tallensi, 161
Tawney, R.H., 34
Tabhaga movement, 99–100
Tepoztlan, 27
Thompson, E.P., 127, 131n, 139
Thorner, D., 26n, 46n, 93
Tolstoy, L., 123n
Tonnies, F., 28, 29, 48
Totemism, 12
Tribe, 17–18; and peasantry, 60–77; concept of, 77–81; Hinduized, 70; Scheduled, 64, 74, 77, 79
Trobriand Islands, 5
Trotskyist, 116, 124, 160
Turgenev, I., 123n

Tylor, E.B., 146n

Uberoi, J.P.S., 81n
Universalization, 38

van Emelen, A., 71n
Vellala, 53, 54
Vico, G., 128
Village studies, 30–41; in China, 30–6, 39, 56–7, 59; in Europe, 40–1; in India, 37–40
Voluntarism, 129, 135

Warner, W.L., 5, 19
Weber, M., 105, 107, 135

Webster, N., 45
White, L.A, 159
Whyte, W.F., 10
Wilson, G., 63
Wilson, M., 63
Wolf, E., 29n, 47, 48
Women, position of, 55–9
Worsley, P., 155, 161

Yalman, N., 58n
Yang, C.K., 35
Yang, M., 33
Yunnan villages, 35–6

Zinoviev, G.Y., 118, 134

LIBRARY OF DAVIDSON COL